A History of the American People

The Colonial Era

A History of the American People

THE

COLONIAL

ERA

HERBERT APTHEKER

INTERNATIONAL PUBLISHERS • NEW YORK

Library of Congress Catalog Card Number 59-11215
ISBN 0-7178-0034-2, 0-7178-0033-4 (pbk)

This Printing, 1979

Second edition, 1966

©1959, BY INTERNATIONAL PUBLISHERS CO., INC.

PRINTED IN THE UNITED STATES OF AMERICA

 209

PREFACE TO THE SECOND EDITION

The book now before the reader, in its second printing, was rarely disturbed by reviews; hence, that the publisher re-issues it is especially gratifying. Among the few reviews that did appear was one by Page Smith, Professor of History at the University of California (Los Angeles), in the *Economic History Review*, published in Holland, (Summer, 1960).

The distinguished biographer of John Adams, in a most generous manner, thought the book "a welcome relief from the 'homogenized history' of recent years." Professor Smith went on to suggest that "dialectical materialism . . . has an old-fashioned charm," and that "it has not been superseded by any newer or more satisfactory system for interpreting our past."

Professor Smith did think that my "constant emphasis on the creative role of the Indian and Negro slave in colonial America" was "simply sentimentality"; he has not, however, persuaded me of this, and I have in no way altered these "sentimental" passages. Indeed, encouraged by Professor Smith's overall conclusion—that the book "gives an informed and intelligent account of our colonial beginnings"—I have made no changes at all in the text.

But the reader is herewith offered a listing of what are considered the most important writings in the area of the colonial period to appear since 1959; the new works listed in the Additional Bibliography (page 153) are distinguished either for their provocative interpretations or their treatment of neglected aspects of that foundation epoch.

June, 1966   *Herbert Aptheker*

Contents

Chapter I

The Beginnings

THE FOUNDING of the colonies which became the United States of America was a consequence of the appearance of capitalism in Europe. In turn, those colonies were an important source of wealth and power for the rulers of the developing European capitalist nations.

England's achievement of economic and naval supremacy in Europe by the 17th century determined the fact that she was to play the decisive role in conquering and colonizing the North American continent. Since supremacy was not achieved until that century, even then remaining a matter of challenge, Spain was able to dominate the southern extremity and France the northern extremity of the continent. But the consolidation of British power saw the complete elimination of Dutch and Swedish colonial competition in America, the ousting of France from Nova Scotia and Canada, and the receding of the Spanish line south of the Floridas.

I

In the early history of capitalism one may discern two fundamental periods: One, in the 17th century, found the feudal system decisively overcome in England, with the Cromwellian Revolution of 1640 its political highlight. Then the newly-ascendant bourgeoisie, frightened by the separatist and levelling demands of the Left wing and of the masses associated in its struggles, compromised the Revolution in the 1660 Restoration by coming to terms with the large landowners. But the Restoration by no means undid the basic nature of the Revolution—that is, its anti-feudal content. When the counter-movement threatened to go too far, the bourgeoisie, stimulated by demonstrations and local uprisings of the poor, led in the "Glorious Revolution" of 1689, where the supremacy of Parliament was confirmed, but not without extending the compromise with the landed aristocracy.

Second, appeared the industrial revolution of the late 18th and early 19th centuries, which accelerated the development of capitalism.

It was within the first stage, and a fragment of the second, that the drama of the colonial period of the United States was enacted. Hence there is the closest economic, political, ideological, and cultural tie between Europe, especially Great Britain, and the colonies, with the subordination of the latter to the former being a decisive feature of early American history.

This does not mean, as the late Edward P. Cheyney put it, over fifty years ago, that, "The history of America is a branch of that of Europe." Nor does it mean, as Daniel J. Boorstin put it, writing in 1958, that colonial development was overwhelmingly, if not exclusively, *American*, so that:[1]

> The more we begin to see the local lineage of their [the Revolutionary Fathers'] ideas, the less we need seek a cosmopolitan philosophical ancestry or try to explain them as ideas which lack a local habitation but are supposed to have been "in the air" all over the world. The motives of the Revolution will dissolve into the commonplace. The philosophers of the European Enlightenment who have been hauled into the court of historians as putative fathers of the Revolution may then seem as irrelevant as the guilty cousin who suddenly appears in the last scene of a bad mystery play.

The truth rather is that there is interpenetration in American colonial development and history between the local scene and its requirements and the imperial scene and its requirements. The peculiarly and particularly American appears and functions within the context of English domination and control; the latter fact has decisive influence upon the nature of colonial development, at the same time as the former fact exerts fundamental influence upon that development. The appearance of the particular does not negate the existence of the general.

There is, moreover, another conclusion frequently drawn from the European origins of the colonies which may be considered here, on the threshold of our work. Again, we may turn to Cheyney's volume for an early and stark expression of this common view: "From the time of the settlement forward, the only population of America that has counted has been of European origins." While nothing quite that neat and blunt is in the recent work of Boorstin, its content is quite within that tradition. That is to say, Boorstin presents the American Indians as obstacles to be overcome, as *objects* of American history. He finds, therefore, any policy posited on their humanity (as that pursued by the Quakers) to have been absurd and costly—he even describes a particular Pennsylvania Indian rising as "the fiery harvest of a half-century of Quaker generosity and non-resistance to the Indians" (p. 58) as though such risings did not occur in areas not "afflicted" with generosity and non-resistance, and as though it were not the white's encroachments and brutality that provoked the resistance of the Indian.

As for that portion of the colonial population which came originally from Africa and not from Europe (and amounted to 20 per cent of the whole population by the time of the Revolution), Boorstin is able to give one sentence, so redolent of ignorance and so permeated by chauvinism, that he could better have spared his readers: "The uncouth Negro slave, only a generation or two from the African jungle, was taught to play the role of peasant" (p. 103).

Actually, from the earliest period, notwithstanding the fact that the impulse toward colonization is European, the process of colonization and the content of its history were significantly influenced by the presence and the activities of the African-derived and the Indian peoples. This is indeed a unique feature of American development, but, though for other purposes Boorstin was anxious to concentrate upon and, indeed, to exaggerate the purely "American" content of United States history, in this respect, he somehow missed an opportunity.

II

In the first and second stages of the history of capitalism, outstanding features of its development were the land-enclosure movement which, with other devices, resulted in dispersing tens of thousands of peasants; the ravishing of Africa, and the enslavement of much of its population; the plundering of America and the enslavement (in certain cases, as in present Haiti, the fairly complete annihilation) of the original inhabitants, and the colonizing of the Western hemisphere for more sustained and systematic exploitation; lastly, the subjugation of Asia with varying degrees of success, but with very high returns in terms of riches and power.

These developments were inter-related; the first three have the closest connection to the beginnings of American history. Let us briefly examine certain aspects of that relationship.

The capitalist revolution was marked by the swift accumulation of fluid capital. To enhance the rate of profit derived from such accumulations and to develop the markets for the products of the rising capitalist economy, overseas enterprises took on special consequence. While in those countries where the break from feudalism was least complete—as in Spain and Portugal—such colonial efforts were made directly under the sponsorship and control of the Crown, in other areas, as in England and Holland, such efforts were made via mixed forms and with varying sponsorship. Thus, in England, there developed Royal colonies, where the direct impact of the Crown was present; Proprietary colonies, where some individual had been granted economic and political rights by the Crown; and Chartered colonies, where joint-stock companies had been granted these rights by the

Crown. In the latter, the greatest degree of separation from monarchical control tended to appear.

In the joint-stock companies, groups of merchants and manufacturers invested varying amounts of capital and shared in the ownership. They evolved from the 15th century Society of Merchant Adventurers, itself reflecting the transition from feudalism to capitalism. This Society was more local in its ventures and represented a significantly lower amount of capitalization; but it did serve as the harbinger of the joint-stock companies.

Such companies first appeared in order to exploit commercial possibilities in northeastern Europe (as the Muscovy company), or the Near East (as the Levant Company), or in Africa (as the Royal African Trading Company). From these it was but a step, given the opening up of the New World, to the formation of joint-stock companies (often with identical personnel) for the penetration and exploitation of America. These companies, as the London Company and the Plymouth Company (taking their names from their home bases), armed with charters from the King, proceeded to colonize their properties with the purpose of profiting therefrom.

The process whereby feudalism was destroyed resulted in the driving from the soil of thousands of serfs and tenants. This uprooting created fierce poverty, widespread unemployment, and wholesale vagabondage. These in turn produced serious social tension and great danger for the rich and their state.

Capitalism's development, however, not only produced this "excess" and dangerous population at home; it also opened up new worlds across the seas. In those new worlds—and in the 16th century, especially in America—were to be found enormous resources and tremendous land surfaces. But with the enormous resources and great land areas, particularly in the northern part of America where England was to concentrate its efforts, there existed a very sparse population, and therefore an insufficient labor supply. Though the resources of that northern hemisphere were believed to be stupendous, they would remain potential so long as the creator of all value, labor power, was not available.

Hence, these two concomitants of the transition from feudalism to capitalism naturally complemented each other, as contemporaries pointed out. Sir Humphrey Gilbert, for example, half brother of Sir Walter Raleigh and a leading soldier and explorer, wrote in 1574:

> We might inhabit some part of these Countryes [in the New World] and settle there such needy people of our country which now trouble the commonwealth and through want here at home are enforced to commit outrageous offences, whereby they are dayly consumed by the gallows.

The Spanish Minister to England reported in 1611 to his Monarch, who was watching English activities with jealous and apprehensive eyes: "Their principal reason for colonizing these parts is to give an outlet to so many idle, wretched people, and thus to prevent the dangers that might be feared of them." Thirteen years later the London Company declared its colonial objective to be: "The removing of the surcharge of necessitous people, the matter or fuel of dangerous insurrections, and thereby leaving the greater plenty to sustain those remaining within the Land." These contemporary statements omitted other important considerations, but they were pointing to one of great moment.

The interpenetration of these historical processes may be illustrated further. Thus, the actual conquest of much of the New World by the Spanish and Portuguese resulted in the flooding of Europe with gold and silver, and the making of extraordinary profits by merchants, who hence derived a capital fund from which they might the more easily venture in additional overseas and colonial investments. Moreover, the increment of enormous profits by merchant families led many of them to invest their excess in textile, leather, wool and metal manufacturing; this, in turn, intensified the shift from a feudal to a capitalist economy and the resulting demand for overseas markets to absorb the products of industry.

But, while the steep rise in prices which accompanied this process helped shoot profits sky-high, it deepened the already impoverished state of the masses, for the real earnings of the poor steadily declined. One set of figures will indicate what was happening: In England, prices rose about 250 per cent from 1501 to 1650, but wages lagged so far behind, that real earnings in 1700 were no more than 50 per cent what they had been in 1500.

No wonder John Winthrop, first Governor of the Massachusetts Bay colony, in explaining the migration from England, said, "This land grows weary of her inhabitants"; and that Queen Elizabeth, after journeying through her realm, cried out, "There are paupers everywhere!"

From the beginning, then, the English colonies served as safety valves for the high social pressures built up by the exploitation and oppression in European states, and this continued well into the twentieth century. England, Scotland, Ireland, France, Germany, Italy, Greece, Sweden, Poland, Russia, and other lands, were the source from whence for centuries millions of working people went West—bringing with them their skills, their strength, and their aspirations.

III

In point of time, the first area outside of Europe to attract the benign eye of acquisitive merchants, the righteous sigh of pious missionaries and the consecrated sword of gracious sovereigns was that land-mass nearest to it, and around which one needs go to reach the fabled riches of Asia—that is, Africa.

The military subjugation of Africa in modern times, and the enslavement of sections of its population, was begun by Portugal in the middle of the 15th century; in the ensuing years Spain, England, France, and Holland joined in the lucrative undertaking.

The beginning of the modern African slave trade preceded Columbus' voyage to the Western world by half a century. It started with Europeans invading the West African coast and seizing its inhabitants, in a rather crude and unorganized fashion, for sale on the European market, especially, in the first years, in Portugal and Spain.

The earliest extant record of a slave-catching expedition is that kept by Azurara, leader of a Portuguese venture in 1446. It is typical of hundreds that were to follow in the generations to come, and we may pause to examine the event as described by its guiding spirit. Azurara's ship made land on the West-Central coast of Africa. Soldiers swarmed ashore, captured a few curious souls, and pressed at once inland seeking more victims. They found a community of people, and for the rest, we turn to the record directly:

> They looked towards the settlement and saw that the Negroes, with their women and children, were already coming as quickly as they could out of their dwellings, because they had caught sight of their enemies. But they [the Portuguese] shouting out "St. James," "St. George," and "Portugal," at once attacked them, killing and taking all they could. Then might you see mothers forsaking their children and husbands their wives, each striving to escape as best he could.
>
> Some drowned themselves in the water; others thought to escape by hiding under their huts; others stowed their children among the sea-weed, where our men found them afterwards, hoping they would thus escape notice. And at last our Lord God who giveth a reward for every good deed, willed that for the toil they had undergone in his service, they should that day obtain victory over their enemies, as well as payment for all their labor and expense; for they took captive of those Negroes, what with men, women, and children, 165, besides those that perished and were killed.

As this quotation indicates, in this business the brutality was rivaled only by the sanctimoniousness. Thus, two of the ships used by Good Queen Bess' favorite naval hero, Sir John Hawkins, in his slave-trading business were called *John the Baptist* and *Jesus*.

This process of rapine and carnage—next to war-making the most profitable of all business endeavors marking the era of capitalism—lasted for over four hundred years; for ferocity it has no peer in all the awful annals of human oppression. And as a central feature of the process of the primitive accumulation of capital, it is a basic component of the history of capitalism, and of American capitalism in particular.

For the first fifty years, this slave-trading business supplied labor for plantations in southern Portugal, for Spanish mines, and for domestic service in those countries and in France and England. Then, with the discovery of the two continents in America whose greatest need was for strong labor familiar to the ways of mining and agriculture, the special function of Africa as a great source for much of that labor was established.

Obviously, from the viewpoint of capitalist economics and ethics, this was to be the role of Africa, and that role was to be of particular importance in North America, especially in what was to become the United States. It was of particular importance there because when the Europeans came there were no more than a million inhabitants ("Indians," the Europeans called them) throughout the area now called Canada and the United States, and probably about 200,000 men, women, and children in the entire area from Maine to Florida and from the ocean to the Appalachian Mountains.

From lack of an indigenous and exploitable population arose the necessity for the mass importation of labor, particularly needed in large numbers in a plantation economy such as was to be established in the favorable climate and terrain found in the zone from present-day Florida to Maryland. A plantation economy, rather than agriculture by numerous freeholders, was of special interest to the rulers of England, because it provided the best means for control of a large labor force needed to produce raw materials missing from the home country.

Such an economy required a numerous, impoverished and relatively unfree labor supply. The home country, and other areas of Europe would supply an important part of that population, especially in the form of indentured servants (of whom more later). But the population of Europe was needed in its largest proportion in Europe; to denude the home continent would be to kill the goose in one wild scramble to gather the golden eggs. Moreover, hundreds of thousands would be needed in the enormous area north of Maryland, where the crops and the form of the economy were to be different.

Slaves could not be imported for labor in English America from the well-populated areas of Central and South America because these lands were already dominated and exploited by Spain and Portugal. There was no possibility of the importation of slaves from Asia because the subjugation of Asia was to occur many generations after Columbus' voyage, and because, in any case, the powers and techniques of the European states were not then developed to the point of coping with the problem of hauling slaves by sea from Asia to America.

Given the conditions which existed in the 16th and 17th centuries one solution was possible and it was undertaken: the conquest and rape of Africa. Here was a continent of about one hundred millions, and one which was near enough to Europe and to America to be manageable in terms of available technique. Here, too, lived millions of people who were in an agricultural stage of civilization, where for centuries cattle had been domesticated, iron had been smelted (probably first in the world), cotton had been woven, soap, glass, pottery, blankets had been made.

And, once enslaved and brought to America, the African, unlike the Indian, would be in a strange country, would not have his people and his social organization to succor him in flight or in resistance. No, once enslaved in Africa and brought to the New World, he would be literally in chains, in a foreign land, thousands of miles from home, and completely in the power of well-armed, ruthless masters, having behind them the full punitive powers of the state.

In the slave-trade business fabulous profits, doubling and quintupling original investments in one or two voyages, were made by the rich of all Europe and, later, by the merchants of the New World, especially those of New England. Ports like Bristol and Liverpool, Perth Amboy and Newport flourished, to a considerable degree, on the basis of the slave trade. In this sense, the enslavement of the African continent was of basic importance in the development of world capitalism, as Africa's intensified exploitation, beginning with the late 19th century, has been of basic consequence in the strength of world imperialism. Indicative of the meaning of this business in money terms is the fact that the value of the over 300,000 slaves hauled in 878 Liverpool ships from 1783 to 1793 was more than 15 million pounds—and that is but one port, for one decade.

To convey the meaning of this business in human terms is very much more difficult. In the four hundred years of the African slave trade something like 15 million Africans were brought, alive, to the Western Hemisphere. For every one who reached these shores alive, about five or six had died—in the wars in Africa, during the trek to the coast, while in the barracoons, waiting for the slave-ships to arrive, in the frequent insurrections aboard ships, and in the course of the horrors of the six or eight or ten weeks of the Middle Passage. Dr. Du Bois, in his classical study of *The Suppression of the African Slave Trade*, stated as one example of the Middle-Passage losses that the Royal African Company shipped about 60,000 slaves from 1680 to 1688, of whom over 14,000 died at sea.

This means that in four centuries, from the 15th through the 19th, Africa lost in enslaved and killed about 65 to 75 million people, and these were a select part of the population, since normally one does not enslave the aged, the lame, the sickly. It is one of the marvels of human history that the peoples of Africa survived this unparalleled ordeal, and that they are today more numerous and more highly organized than ever before and are, indeed, on the threshold of full national liberation.

But, of course, the heart of Africa's contribution to the development of European capitalism and of the American colonies —and of American capitalism—does not lie in the slave *trade,* profitable as that was. It lies rather in slavery, in the unpaid and forced labor of millions of Negroes for over two centuries.

In explaining the speed and magnitude of the growth of American capitalism, historians have pointed, correctly, to several factors: the tremendous size and fabulous resources of the United States; its separation from the continual and devastating wars of Europe, which set back its competitors and from which the U.S. bourgeoisie reaped huge profits; the immigration, for generations, of millions of Europeans, Asians, and Latin-Americans with their skills and strength (and their differences, making their domination and exploitation easier); the prolonged existence of a bourgeois-democratic republic, an ideal state form for the early development and maturing of capitalism. All these are consequential, and we shall have occasion to refer to them again as our story unfolds.

But of as much consequence as any one of these, was the fact that within the borders of the developing American capitalism there lived for almost three hundred years a significant fraction of the population (from 10 to 20 per cent of the whole) which was nakedly enslaved. Under these conditions, exploitation reached its most intense form, and these millions of workers produced profits running into the multi-billions from the cotton, sugar, rice, tobacco, hemp, gold, coal, and lumber their labor created. All this is quite beside the value Negro slavery represented to the rulers of the country in terms of hamstringing the labor movement and bulwarking reaction generally.

The matter is complex, however, for in terms of the fullest *development* of capitalism, slavery became a central obstacle; but in terms of the economic conquest of this continent, and of the early accumulation of capital, the enslavement of the Negro people was organic to the appearance and rise of American capitalism.

IV

As a rule, English policy toward the people originally inhabiting the colonized areas was one of genocide. Two great groupings of peoples occupied the area which was to make up the thirteen colonies; these were the Iroquois and the Algonkian, and they totalled some 200,000 souls. Their culture was of the Stone Age, and their only domesticated animal was the dog.

They lived by hunting and fishing and by a very extensive form of farming; much of the labor, and some of the governing, was done by women.

Land was held in common and only hunting rights to particular areas might accrue to certain groups and might be alienated by treaty. Chiefs were not comparable to European kings; rather, they were elder statesmen whose influence came from demonstrated ability and character; their decisions were never personal and never binding unless collectively affirmed. (The white interlopers refused to comprehend these social institutions and preferred to view Indian society in terms of European laws and mores—a distortion that frequently was the source of the rationalizations for denouncing new "evidences" of Indian "deceit.")

The British rulers came from a society in which the lives of their own subjects (especially if poor) were evaluated very cheaply; thus, the theft of a loaf of bread was a capital crime. This inhumanity—mirroring an acquisitive society—showed itself at its worst when confronted by the Indian. For here was a people, having possession of wealth and land coveted by the invaders, who, heathen that they were, betrayed a fanatical disregard for the obviously superior rights of devout and white Christians.

Mark Twain described the result in a sentence: the pious interlopers, he wrote, "first fell on their knees, and then on the aborigines." No method was too horrible for the accomplishment of the governmental policy of subjugation and extermination. These methods ran the gamut from rewards of so many pounds per scalp of Indian man, woman, or child, to bacteriological warfare in the form of spreading blankets infected with small-pox germs. Of innumerable examples of early capitalist methods of conquest, two must suffice:

The first comes from Governor Bradford of the Plymouth Colony. He is writing of an attack on the Pequots in 1637 on the banks of the Mystic River; it was marked by the burning of Indian homes:

It is a fearful sight to see them frying in the fire and the streams of blood quenching the same and horrible was the stink and stench thereof. But the victory seemed a sweet sacrifice and they gave praise thereof to God.

The other example—and both are altogether characteristic—comes from the history of the Dutch Governor Kieft of New Amsterdam (later New York) who decided, in 1643, on an effort to wipe out the Indians in the environs of Manhattan. Without warning one night, he sent soldiers to attack a Raritan village. David de Vries, a leader among the Dutch colonists, was with the Governor that night. He wrote:

I heard a great shrieking, and I ran to the ramparts of the fort . . . . Saw nothing but firing, and heard the shrieks of the savages murdered in their sleep . . . . When it was day the soldiers returned to the fort, having massacred eigthy Indians, and considering they had done a deed of Roman valor . . . . Infants were torn from their mothers' breasts and hacked to pieces in the presence of the parents, and the pieces were thrown into the fire and in the water, and other sucklings, being bound to small boards, were cut, stuck, pierced, and miserably massacred in a manner to move a heart of stone. Some were thrown into the river, and when the fathers and mothers endeavored to save them, the soldiers would not let them come on land but made both parties and children drown.

Nothing is beyond rationalization; for this, too, contemporaries had convincing explanations. Thus, Robert Gray, writing in 1609 a very early piece of "promotional" literature, *A Good Speed to Virginia,* declared:

The earth . . . which is man's fee-simple by deeds of gift from God, is the greater part of it possessed and wrongfully usurped by wild beasts, and unreasonable creatures, or by brutish savages, which by reason of their godless ignorance, and blasphemous idolatrie, are worse than those beasts which are of a most wild and savage nature.

More devastating to the Indians, however, than the bullets and fire of the European, were the diseases which he brought and against which the Indian had developed no immunity. Thus, for instance, two years before the Pilgrims came to Plymouth, most of the Indians in present New England had died of a plague probably contracted from fishermen off the coast of Maine. It was the cornfields of a nearly annihilated tribe that the Pilgrims appropriated upon their arrival.

The white colonizers, then, brought the Indians death and destruction, and met a persistent and heroic resistance which constitutes one of the great sagas of human history. It is, however, a tragic saga, for the Indians, divided amongst themselves, generally outnumbered, tremendously out-armed, and terribly prone to the new diseases brought by the invader from Europe, went down to defeat. Let it be noted, that where some decency and honor prevailed—as in the cases of William Penn and Roger Williams—the Indians maintained fraternal relations with the whites.

From the Indians, on the other hand, the colonizing powers obtained not only their land and wealth, but also skills and techniques without which the whole colonizing effort must have failed. Some of this was the result of the conflict itself—notably a new way of waging war, which, in the days of the Revolution, was to be decisive in the winning of independence. But most of the contributions came as free-will offerings of helpfulness.

Thus, it was the Indians who taught the newcomers how to clear the primeval forest and prepare the land for cultivation. They taught the whites how to plant corn and tobacco, peas and beans, pumpkins and squash, melons and cucumbers; how to make maple-sugar; how fish-heads might be used as fertilizer; how to trap and hunt the wild animals and how to dress their skins; how to make the birch-bark canoe (without which the wilderness could never have been penetrated); how to bake the clams on the beach. The trails of the Indians were the paths of the colonists (as so many of them were to become the roads of the automobile age). In a word, the Indians taught the Europeans how to live in the New World, and were repaid by having that World taken away from them.[2]

Chapter II

The Colonial Relationship

AMERICAN HISTORY DURING the century and a half that culminates in the revolutionary upheaval has several persistent themes. Dominant, of course, is the colonial relationship vis-á-vis England. Another consequential facet of the period's history is the working out of Great Power rivalries (especially those of England, France, Spain and Holland). Indian relations form an additional decisive feature of the epoch.

At the same time, the development of an indigenous socio-economic order, with the problems of advancing agriculture, commerce and industry, the appearance and growth of classes—propertied and unpropertied—with competition and conflict among them, are fundamental to the period. As part of this, but having special characteristics and importance, was the institution of chattel slavery, with its impact on law, ideology, mores, and with its own content in terms of the unique experience and efforts of the Negro slaves.

Moreover, a consequence of the particular history of the colonial peoples in the course of 150 years, is the development of a new nationality—the American—the assertion of which was to be so basic a component of the American Revolution.

I

Sir Walter Raleigh (1552-1613) declared: "Who rules the trade of the world rules the wealth of the world and consequently the world itself."

Each of the major powers of western Europe set itself the objective of making itself supreme within the circle of its own competitors. To achieve this meant to overcome the rival in war, to surpass him in the effective exploitation of the home population, to secure ownership over as much of the land mass of the world as possible (and to take away whatever the rival himself was able first to appropriate). Colonies would be sources of wealth for the rulers of the metropolitan power, and bases from which additional conquests might be launched.

The colonization program was central to the whole effort at supremacy. The more colonies you had, the less had the opponent. The colonies were sources of raw materials, and owning them relieved one of dependence upon foreign powers who hitherto had served as the suppliers. The colonies were fountains of enormous wealth, directly in terms of their products, as lumber, fur, gold, naval stores, fish, tobacco, indigo, rice, etc., and somewhat less directly through the profits to be made by trade in these thousand and one precious commodities. The colonies were sources of manpower for the armies and navies. The colonies were markets wherein might be sold, at high profits, the slaves to produce many of the enriching commodities, and the manufactured goods that they would need but that they would be forbidden to make themselves. As industry developed in England, especially during the 18th century, this latter motive became more and more impelling.

From the viewpoint, then, of the rulers of England, the colonies were planted and existed for the purpose of enriching those rulers and enhancing their power. Adam Smith, concentrating on the economic aspects, wrote in his *Wealth of Nations* (1776), that England "had founded a great empire for the sole purpose of raising up a people of customers." Her merchants had seen to it, he declared, that English laws gave them a monopoly of American trade, forcing the colonists to buy from them and to sell to them; in both instances they set the prices, high in the former case and low in the latter. "The maintenance of this monopoly," wrote Smith, "has hitherto been the principal, or more properly perhaps the sole end and purpose of the dominion which Great Britain assumes over her colonies."

A pioneer British empire promoter, Richard Hakluyt, publishing *A Discourse on Western Planting* in 1586, concentrated on another central advantage accruing to the rulers through the vigorous pursuit of a colonization policy. Such a policy, he held, was vital in challenging the supremacy of Spain in Europe, for the power of the Spanish monarch rested on the wealth he drained from America. "Entering into the consideration of how this [King] Philip may be abased," wrote Hakluyt, "I mean first to begin with the West Indies, as there to lay a foundation for his overthrow." After Spain it was Holland and France. In this sense the colonists existed as pawns wherewith to help fight Britain's battle for world supremacy, and very many colonists expired as cannon-fodder in intermittent wars, whose real source lay in the ambition and rapacity of men residing thousands of miles away.

Once the appearance of capitalism had set in motion the process of colonization, the two became intertwined. One's growth accentuated the other's; but always the relationship was parasitic, with the colonies the victims. Thus, as an instance: the major industries of 17th century England were the making of iron and copper, the building of ships, and the production of woolens. For all these, wood was vital. But wood was exactly what England did not have. She resented and lamented her dependence upon the Baltic countries for this product; wars on sea and land frequently cut off this source, in any case. Without wood, there was no timber for the ships, and no resin, tar and pitch to make the ships watertight; without wood, there was no fuel (at that period) for the iron and copper furnaces; without wood there was neither potash nor dyes for the woolen factories. And the colonies, from New England to Georgia, abounded in lumber.

Another instance: as capitalism developed in England, the markets of Europe became more and more consequential to her. This need for additional markets was intensified in the England of the early 17th century, because the persistence of feudal relationships in many areas severely limited the absorbing capacity of the home market. At the same period, however, the markets provided by continental Europe were becoming less and less dependable because other rising national bourgeoisies on the continent sought to exclude foreign competitors and because that mainland was rent by continual wars. Thus, the Thirty Years' War, beginning in 1618, cut off many markets for English goods, and helped produce a severe depression in England that persisted throughout the 1620's. This, in turn, helped direct the gaze of the English ruling circles toward the West.

As industry develops in England, and capitalist *production* becomes decisive, the colonial policy appropriate for an earlier period, when a merchant bourgeoisie allied with a land-based nobility were dominant, is more and more persistently and successfully questioned. This development becomes prominent by the end of the 17th century and is of increasing consequence throughout the 18th century. It is fundamental to the growing splits in English ruling circles, both in terms of the two revolutions of the 17th century, and of the sharp conflicts that develop later over the internal and colonial policies of George III.

These shifts and struggles within English political circles have the most direct bearing upon colonial history; they are of decisive importance in explaining the numerous colonial insurrections that mark the 17th century (as we shall see), and the less violent but no less consequential political divisions that mark the 18th century and that culminate in 1775 in the greatest explosion of all.

While the colonies were viewed by the rulers of England as areas to be exploited and as bases to further their ambitions for power, they were viewed otherwise, quite naturally, by the colonists themselves. Some of these colonists were servitors, officials or flunkeys of the imperial power and their interests coincided, of course. But the overwhelming majority of them—propertied and non-propertied—viewed the colonies as their home (even if for decades many spoke of England, or other parts of Europe, as Home). They had hazarded their lives in crossing the Atlantic

with the idea of improving those lives—always excepting, of
course, those forcibly transported. The purpose of the colonizers
was to exploit the colonists; this meant a direct and fundamental
conflict of interests that could be resolved only by the elimination
of the exploiting interest.

The matter can be put no more neatly than it was by a British
contemporary, the Marquis of Carmathen, in speaking to the
House of Lords. "For what purpose," he asked, "were they [the
colonists] suffered to go to that country unless the profits of their
labor should return to their masters here? I think the policy of
colonization is highly culpable if the advantage of it should not
redound to the interests of Great Britain."

When one points to this basic conflict between the colonizers
and the colonists, he is not necessarily maintaining that the latter
consciously objected to the theoretical assumptions of mercantilism. The great authorities in colonial history, George L. Beer
and Charles M. Andrews, were both insistent that the colonists
did not, in the early period, question the prevalent economic
theories and that one must not, with hindsight, read such understanding into their minds. Certainly, the working out of a mature
theoretical challenge to the dominant views of the mercantilistic
writers took several generations, but this arose on the basis of the
existing *real* contradictions of interest, without which conflicting
theories would not and could not have developed.

In planting colonies, the rulers planted rebellion. The rebellion
was organic to the contradictory interests of the colonizers and
the colonists. Its seeds were nurtured in the distance between
colonists and rulers; in the mixture of peoples that produced a
new people as the decades passed; in the separate experiences of
the colonists that united them among themselves and increasingly
severed them from Home; in the distinct economies of the
colonies that, despite obstructions and restrictions, did develop;
in the common feeling of dissatisfaction and exploitation and
"separateness" that, together with everything else, made of them
another people.

II

Administratively, colonial affairs were controlled in London by the Board of Trade. Legislatively, Parliament, of course, was supreme and the colonies were unrepresented, though as early as 1698, an official told the King that many Rhode Islanders were asserting that "no law of England ought to be in force and binding to them without their consent for they foolishly say they have no representatives sent from themselves to the Parliament in England."

Even in strictly internal affairs, English administrative fetters were notable. Thus, colonial assemblies, though succeeding by struggles that paralleled those waged by the English Parliament against the King in enhancing their local powers, never were allowed to choose their own speakers, to over-ride the governor's veto, to fix regular elections, or to establish new election districts. Moreover, laws passed by the colonial assemblies were subject to final review by the Board of Trade, and that body (or its equivalent under other names) actually did veto over five hundred laws passed by the colonies from 1675 to 1775. And in all cases, criminal and civil (including, in the latter, cases involving land ownership) the court of last appeal was the King.

There is a passage in Jefferson's *Autobiography* which is particularly revealing of the realities of colonial politics, and cuts through questions of formal requirements. It is fairly long, but repays careful reading:

> In 1769 I became a member of the legislature by choice of the county in which I live, and so continued until it was closed by the Revolution. I made one effort in that body for the permission of the emancipation of the slaves, which was rejected: and indeed, during the regal government, nothing liberal could expect success. Our minds were circumscribed within narrow limits, by an habitual belief that it was our duty to be subordinate to the mother country in all matters of government, to direct all our labors in subservience to her interests, and

even to observe a bigoted intolerance for all religions but hers.
The difficulties with our representatives were of habit and
despair, not of reflection and conviction. Experience soon
proved that they could bring their minds to rights, on the first
summons of their attention. But the King's Council, which
acted as another house of the legislature, held their places at
will, and were in most humble obedience to that will: the
Governor, too, who had a negative on our laws, held by the
same tenure, and with still greater devotedness to it, and, last
of all, the Royal negative closed the door to every hope of
amelioration.

But it was in economic matters that imperial interference was
most notable. The interference was directed towards making of
the colonies suppliers of raw materials and consumers of finished
products. This carried with it, in certain cases, bounties and other
rewards; but, on the whole, it meant a severe inhibition upon
the development of a rounded American economy.

The laws took three main forms: regulating trade, limiting
industry, and curbing the emission of currency. All had the objective of keeping the American economy subordinate to and
dependent upon that of Great Britain.

The laws regulating trade (basic was the Navigation Act of
1660) provided generally for England's monopolization of the
carrying and merchandising of colonial products (and of English goods destined for the colonies). These trade acts resulted in
a heavy indirect tax upon the colonists because of an unfavorable
balance of trade. For the years 1700 through 1773, the excess of
imports from England over exports to her from the colonies totalled more than 20 million pounds, a colossal sum for those days
and one which helped decisively in sustaining the power of the
British ruling class.

Laws dealing with industry (such as the Wool Act, 1699, the
Hat Act, 1732, the Iron Act, 1750) generally forbade the colonists from engaging in manufacturing (especially the finished-prod-
uct stage of manufacturing). Even William Pitt, who favored a
conciliatory policy towards the colonies, in his speech urging the
repeal of the Stamp Act, declared: "If the Americans should

manufacture a lock of wool or a horseshoe, he would fill their ports with ships and their towns with troops."

Laws dealing with currency finally reached the point of flatly prohibiting its issuance by the colonies. The consequent scarcity of currency retarded colonial economic development and the deflationary policy tended to favor the English creditor over the American, continually in debt.

Even before her enactments outlawing the issuance of colonial currency, England had passed legislation heavily favoring the British creditor over the colonial debtor. This was especially true of an Act of 1732, notably onerous to the perennially indebted tobacco planter, which provided that an affidavit from a resident in England was to have as much weight in court as evidence given in open court and subject to cross-examination; and which added that land and personal estate (including slaves) were to be liable for debt payments in the same manner as was real estate in England. All colonial petitions pleading for repeal of this enactment were rejected in London, and colonial laws relaxing bankruptcy requirements, or in other ways tending to favor debtors, were uniformly vetoed by the King.

British restrictions on the lumber industry were also keenly resented by the colonists. English law attempted to preserve the larger trees for the King's navy, and Royal foresters were provided for the purpose of marking such trees as were *verboten* to the Americans. The laws provoked continual turmoil and were persistently broken—the Massachusetts Assembly in 1720 trying to justify illegality by declaring that the trees in question were the King's only while standing; once cut, said the Assembly with a straight face, they belonged to the colonists!

While England encouraged the colonies in the production of raw materials she herself could not raise, such as rice and indigo, she discouraged the exportation from the colonies to England of products also originating at home. Thus, by the provisions of the so-called Corn Laws, the importation into England of cereals and meats from the colonies was either absolutely barred or, through excessive duties, in fact prohibited; again, a very discriminatory duty was placed upon whale oil and blubber, if brought to England in colonial vessels.

Furthermore, the British Crown regularly disallowed colonial acts seeking to advance manufacturing. For example, the Privy Council disallowed a Pennsylvania law (1705) to encourage shoe manufacture; a New York act (1706) in connection with the making of sailcloth; and a Massachusetts effort to encourage the making of linen (1756). The Board of Trade, which recommended policy to the Privy Council, stated, in 1756: "The passing of laws in the plantations for encouraging manufactures, which in any ways interfere with the manufacture of this kingdom has always been thought improper, and has ever been discouraged."

England also systematically followed a policy of trying to prevent the westward expansion of the colonists. This was done because of English efforts to discourage American speculative efforts in western lands; because of English efforts to monopolize the very profitable Indian fur trade; and because England feared that westward expansion of the American population would make the maintenance of colonial power increasingly difficult and tend to develop a sense of American independence.

The most notable instance of English prohibition of westward movement was the act of 1763 which forbade settlement by the colonists west of the Appalachians. In this all the factors mentioned above were at work and a particularly clear contemporaneous acknowledgment of some of the British motives is at hand. In May, 1763, Lord Egremont, the Secretary of State, explained his favoring the proposed Line of 1763 to Lord Shelburne, President of the Board of Trade, by writing:

> As their [the colonists'] numbers increased, they would emigrate to Nova Scotia or the provinces of the Southern Quarter [the Floridas]—where they would be useful to their Mother Country instead of planting themselves in the heart of America, out of reach of Government where from the great difficulties of procuring European commodities, they would be compelled to commerce and manufactures to the infinite prejudices of Britain.

There was difference of opinion, it is true, among leading English figures on this question of westward expansion. Some held that it should be encouraged, for it tended to disperse the population and in that way would discourage manufacturing. This group did not prevail; but note that the difference was over tactics, not over the goal sought—namely, to prevent the development of American manufacturing.

III

Throughout the sixteen decades of colonial history, war, not peace, was usual. The wars were mainly of three kinds: wars between the colonizing powers, especially England against France; wars of expropriation and extermination fought against various Indian peoples; and civil wars. The last shall be considered when dealing with the internal colonial scene.

Of wars with the Indians, the colonies were never really free. These wars were, of course, the results of aggressions by the whites and resistance by the Indians; they were the result of the whites' policy of land theft, trading swindles, and genocide. In evaluating these wars, it is important to remember that the Indians were always far from numerous—thus, the Iroquois confederation, perhaps the most powerful of all Indian forces east of the Mississippi, never numbered more than 16,000 men, women, and children. Nevertheless, so fierce was the resistance that at times the issue itself was in doubt; had the Indians ever succeeded in welding unity amongst themselves it is certain that their conquest would have been delayed by many years, if not generations.

In evaluating these wars, too, the question of progress arises. It is clear that the productive capacity of the European civilization was much higher than that of the Indians'; certainly the level of the former was higher than that of the latter. Basically, because of the resultant more advanced technique, the European was able to conquer the Indian, even fighting on the Indians' home ground. But of great importance in evaluating the nature of the capitalism which accomplished this conquest, is the manner of the conquest: utterly ruthless, hypocritical, and brutal. These characteristics of the system adhere to it at all stages of its development, from the nature of its American Indian policy when it is young, to the nature of its imperialist policy when it is aged.

In the colonial period mention may be made of four major Indian wars. The Pequot Indians, numbering some 3,000 altogether, rose up in 1637, in Connecticut, in an effort to stop persistant encroachments on their land. The guns of the colonists very nearly annihilated them, the pitiful handful of survivors being sold as slaves in the West Indies.

In 1675, Metacom, leader of the Wampanoag Indians of New England (called by the English, King Philip) succeeded in forging unity with the Nipmuck and Narragansett Indians and offering resistance to further English advances. The struggle lasted for two years, and, seeing his forces growing thinner, Metacom tried to get the Mohawks to join with him. His efforts failed and this sealed the doom of his struggle, for against him the colonists stood united in the New England Confederation. In 1676 he was himself killed, and his body was then drawn and quartered, while his head was displayed on a pole in Plymouth. His wife and boy were sold in West Indian slavery. By 1677, these Indians had been defeated and, indeed, organized Indian tribal life in southern New England was just about wiped out.

Another major war, with similar results, was waged by Cherokee Indians in South Carolina from 1760 through 1762. Finally, after the British betrayal of the Algonkian peoples in the treaty of 1763, concluding the Anglo-French Seven Years' War, several tribes amongst them, led by Pontiac, chief of the Ottawas (joined by the Wyandot, Potawatomi, and Ojibwa) declared war upon the English, and the impact was felt far beyond the Ohio Valley into Pennsylvania, Maryland, and Virginia. This war, starting in 1763, ended with the defeat of Pontiac in 1766.

IV

There were four major wars waged in the colonies as parts of greater ones fought in Europe (and elsewhere) between France and England (with Spain occasionally allied to France). Indeed, from 1689 through 1763 war was practically incessant between these two rapacious powers, but there are four particular outbreaks that may be identified and that cost thousands of lives in French Canada and English America. In all of these, it may be added, Indians participated as allies of one side or the other and much of the fighting took on the character of Indian wars so far as the colonists were concerned, yet Indian wars proper were something additional.

From 1688 through 1697, King William's War—known in Europe as the War of the Grand Alliance—ravaged the northern colonies. From 1701 through 1713 Queen Anne's War—in Europe, the War of the Spanish Succession—was fought.[1] From 1745 through 1748, in the South, occurred the War of Jenkin's Ear, part of the larger War of the Austrian Succession. Finally, the greatest of them all, started in the colonies in 1754, and spreading two years later in Europe as the Seven Years War (1756-1763), is known in colonial history as the French and Indian War.

It is this war which resulted in British acquisition of Canada (some British statesmen weighed taking the French sugar island of Guadeloupe—it was one or the other and the final choice here is reflective of the development of English *industry,* as compared with commerce). At the same time the British betrayed their Indian supporters—led by Pontiac—and in the treaty of peace asserted ownership of the land north of the Ohio river, which was that of their "allies."

This last war had profound repercussions on the further development of colonial history. It intensified British-American land speculations in the West. By removing the French enemy, it made the colonists feel less dependent upon the military might of Eng-

land. By raising to then unprecedented heights the national debt
of England (as Shaw noted, everything in England is Royal, except the debt!) it helped provoke an increasingly onerous taxation
and trade policy toward the colonies on the part of Great Britain,
just when those colonies had become more numerous, more highly
commercialized and more independent in a military, economic
and psychological sense from England than ever before.

While the total casualties in these wars amounted to hardly
more than those sustained in one campaign of a modern war,
they did represent a considerable percentage of the total adult
male population and repeatedly caused grief and dislocation for
the inhibitants. Increasingly these slaughters were resented by the
colonists as resulting not directly from their own needs or interests
but from those of the rulers of England.

Indeed, as far back as 1652, Massachusetts had declared her
neutrality in the Anglo-Dutch War. As the decades passed, this
sense of American separateness grew so that, as the English his-
torian, George Trevelyan, has put it, it was felt "that the burdens
of patriotism were imposed by England and the West Indies but
borne by . . . North America, and that America might not always find it convenient to fight in England's wars."

Relevant is the fact that during the last of the colonial wars—
the Seven Years' War, ending in 1763—the English authorities
had the greatest difficulties in recruiting soldiers within the colonies, and met little cooperation in such efforts from the provincial
legislatures. Attempts to conscript indentured servants were met
with armed resistance by the planters employing them in several
counties in Maryland; some draftees forcibly resisted conscription
in New York. In North Carolina, though the assembly did pass
legislation permitting the drafting of unmarried men, "they,"
wrote Eugene I. McCormac, in a book devoted to *Colonial
Opposition to Imperial Authority during the French and Indian
War,* "avoided the draft by open defiance or hiding." Professor
McCormac continued: "County officials neglected or refused to
make proper returns to the governor, thereby aiding delinquents
and nullifying the laws in a great measure."

Chapter III

Class Conflict at Home

CURTIS P. NETTELS, in his valuable
study of colonial life, *The Roots of American Civilization,* aptly
wrote "of the conflict between privileged and non-privileged
groups—a prolonged strife which forms the central theme of
colonial history." We turn now to an examination of the class
struggles which formed this central theme.

I

First, some remarks about the general nature of colonial society
are in order. Throughout the era, of course, American society was
predominantly rural. This does not mean that cities were not a
significant feature of the American colonial scene; they were as,
notably, Carl Bridenbaugh has been at pains to demonstrate. But
it does mean that the five chief cities of the colonies (Philadelphia, New York, Boston, Charles Town, and Newport, ranging
in population in that order from almost 24,000 to about 7,500)[1]
had altogether less than 73,000 inhabitants in 1760 when the
total population was over 1,600,000.

Tremendously rapid population growth is a marked feature of
colonial history. Excluding Indians, there were 2,500 persons in
the colonies in 1620; 114,000 in 1670; nearly 300,000 in 1720;
and over 2,500,000 (with some 500,000 Negro slaves) in 1775.
And by that last date about one-third of the white population
was non-English in origin.

Throughout the era a considerable fraction of the white population consisted of indentured servants; at any given moment from 10 to 15 per cent of the total was in this condition. This bound and unpaid labor was of two major kinds, voluntary and involuntary. The first was the more numerous and consisted of redemptioners and apprentices. The redemptioners bound themselves as servants (for from two to seven years, with four being most common) in return for passage to the New World. It is estimated that about 70 per cent of all immigration to the colonies down to the Revolution consisted of these redemptioners. Apprentices were children (of the poor) who in return for training gave their services, usually until they were 21 years old. Some impoverished and homeless children of England were shipped to the colonies by the authorities as "bound apprentices."

Less numerous, but still amounting to scores of thousands, were the involuntary indentured servants. These consisted of four groups, two originating in the colonies and two from overseas. The first category was composed of those held to service in lieu of being imprisoned for debt (it must be remembered that jailing for non-payment of debt persisted in some states to the Civil War) and of those held to service in place of sentences imposed by colonial courts for criminal offenses, especially theft and unlawful absence from the employer.

The second category was made up of victims of kidnaping, generally the children of the very poor; and of British convicts spared death or long prison sentences by choosing transportation and servitude (for from 7 to 14 years, a few for life) in the colonies. Some indication of the numbers involved in these two types is provided by the fact that kidnaping was a well organized "racket" (as we would say today) in England and the Continent, with one professional "crimp" boasting that he had succeeded in spiriting away 500 children annually for a dozen years. As for British transportation of criminals—most of whom had been convicted of petty theft induced by extreme poverty and some of whom were political prisoners[2]—the best estimate is that

50,000 men and women were involved up to 1775, the great majority being sent to Virginia and to Maryland.

Unfree labor—Negro and white—which formed so very considerable a section of the entire working population, existed in order to solve a pressing problem confronting the bourgeoisie in developing a vast colonial area. That problem was how to exploit the illimitable resources of the area in face of the fact that that labor power had—in the millions of acres of public and fertile nearby land—the wherewithal itself to get property and with property, get "independence." And independence meant their withdrawal from the labor market, the elimination of that source of surplus value, and the resulting tendency to raise the rate of wages for those not yet propertied. Under such conditions, wrote Marx, in *Capital* (volume I, chapter 25, "Modern Theory of Colonization"):

> What scope is there for the production of superflous wage workers in proportion to the accumulation of capital? The wage worker of today will tomorrow become an independent peasant or handicraftsman, working on his own account. When this happens, he disappears from the labor market—but not into the workhouse. This continuous transformation of wage workers into independent producers, who work for themselves instead of working for capital, and enrich themselves instead of enriching his worship the capitalist, has an injurious reaction upon the state of the labor market.

Hence the absolutely vital nature of the land question for American history until well past the colonial period. Related to this were the swift efforts of the rich to further enrich themselves through the accumulation of vast holdings in the public lands. Much of this represented more or less legitimate speculations and business ventures. But a good deal of it resulted from the action of corrupted colonial (and later state and federal) governments, instruments of the rich, in making huge land grants to the "leading families" (by 1698, New York had given thousands of acres to the Philipses, Van Cortlandts, Van Rensselaers, Schuylers, Livingstons and Bayards; by 1754, Virginia had given almost three million acres to the Carters, Beverleys, and Pages)—an early example of government "aid" to businessmen.

In terms of the early accumulation of capital by the bourgeoisie, outright thievery and corruption were quite notable. Other legal sources—as enslavement and wars of conquest—have been commented upon; illegal and quasi-legal forms, like piracy, were also significant. Cyrus H. Karraker indeed has demonstrated, as the title of his work asserts, that *Piracy Was A Business,* especially in the late 17th and early 18th centuries. Charles M. Andrews—far from a muckraker—in the fourth volume of his *Colonial Period of American History,* wrote there was "an immense amount of thievery going on . . . and that manipulation in the interest of private gain must have been the rule rather than the exception." He found, in fact, "systematic corruption in high places" to have been characteristic throughout the colonial epoch.

It is, nevertheless, a fact that class elasticity was greater in colonial America than it was in contemporaneous England, always excepting the hundreds of thousands who were chattel slaves. It is also a fact that free labor in the colonies did earn in real wages perhaps 30 to 40 per cent more than their class brothers overseas. In saying this it is to be added that these are comparative statements only and that in an absolute sense, to move out of poverty was very difficult in colonial America, and the actual standard of living of the free working people was low—not least because of the competition offered by the large number of workers who were completely unpaid.

Actual figures are sparse and not too meaningful in present-day terms. In New England, unskilled and skilled free workers were paid from 25¢ to about 85¢ a day, depending upon craft and time. Periods of depression and unemployment (and they were frequent in the colonial period) resulted in actual starvation for some, and emergency public relief measures for others. In "good" times, the normal level was just about subsistence.

II

Chattel slavery was less significant than indentured servitude during the 17th century. Thus, as late as 1683, there were 3,000 slaves in Virginia and 12,000 indentured servants. Not until 1710 did rice—overwhelmingly grown by slave labor—become the staple crop of South Carolina; up to that time her leading exports had been deerskins, pork, corn, lumber and naval stores. Georgia was not founded until the 1730's, and slavery was not introduced into that colony (a buffer between Spanish Florida and the English Carolinas) until 1750.

But with the 18th century, and the production of rice, indigo, and tobacco in huge quantities, slave labor became of decisive consequence for all the colonies from Maryland to Georgia. The slaves equalled almost 40 per cent of the total southern population, and 20 per cent of the entire colonial population by the time of the Revolution.

By about 1720, American Negro slavery was a well-developed, single-crop, commodity-producing, commercialized system of enslavement. It already had passed out of the household form into that of the plantation, where commodities were produced for sale in an extensive and world-wide market. This, plus the racist ideology that rationalized and sustained the system, account for the intense exploitation and brutality that characterized the American Negro slave system by the early 18th century and was to characterize it for another 15 decades. Furthermore, already this early in the colonial period, the institution was a basic source of wealth for the planters of the South and for the merchants of the North.

In the southern colonies (particularly after the 17th century) the slaveowning planters—among whom the really influential families were very few and were inter-related—constituted the ruling class. In the Middle and New England colonies, the merchants and the larger landowners (the latter especially important in New York) composed the dominant oligarchy. All these were not the final masters in their own homes, however, since they constituted a colonial dominant group, and ultimate political, military, and economic power rested with the rulers of England, whose direct representatives in the colonies represented the peak of "Society."

The merchant aristocracy was, like that of the planters, few and here, too, there was much intermarriage. It constituted an articulate, closely-knit, and powerful class. In the five leading cities of the colonies, this stratum did not count as many as four hundred families. Its members, however, had direct ties to the governors, they sat on the colonial councils and assemblies, they acquired vast landed estates in deals and through special favors, they consorted with pirates (who, on retiring, sometimes graduated into respectable merchants), waxed fat on the slave trade, made an honest penny by trading with friend or foe during war, and paid their seamen and workers starvation wages. In a word, they were the pillars of society, and their riches certified them, said their ministers, to be the elect of God, as it entitled them to be the rulers of men.

Many branched out in their business interests, especially as the colonial period was drawing to a close, not only into land speculations, but also into the fur trade and industry, particularly shipbuilding and certain subsidiary or processing activities such as flour-milling, brewing and barrel-making.

Finally, constituting perhaps 60 per cent of the total colonial population, were the great mass of more or less independent yeomanry and small farmers and squatters and fishermen. These, together with the unfree and the urban workers—and borrowing heavily from the Indians—made what became the United States.

They expected little and had the modesty characteristic of workers. They had large families, heavy responsibilities, much harassment and few pleasures except such as the poor make for themselves everywhere. They were the salt of the earth and they made our country.

They were far from complacent. They were victimized but

they gave their tormenters a battle and slowly, almost impercep-
tibly, despite innumerable setbacks, they did forge ahead. These
class struggles form the heart of the history of the American
people during the colonial period—as since.

Briefly, we turn to the highlights of this story.

III

First, as to the Negro slaves, of whom, it will be recalled, there
were about half a million by 1775. Here one is dealing with a
system of commodity production for a world market in which the
power of the employer is not more limited than his avaricious-
ness. By law, the slave's submission had to be perfect and the
employer's power absolute, extending to life and limb. And, by
law, this condition was perpetual and accrued to the descend-
ants of both.

The system of slavery was brutality personified and while it
was torture to the male slaves, its impact upon the female really
defies the power of language.

To convey to the reader something of the reality of slavery, in
the colonial period, we shall offer relevant extracts from the
diary of William Byrd of Virginia (1674-1744). This Mr. Byrd
owned over 170,000 acres of land (it was on one of his estates
that the city of Richmond was laid out); he was a member of
the Virginia Council for over 30 years; he was the owner of a
library of some 4,000 volumes, was a noted art connoisseur, and
a distinguished author. This Mr. Byrd, indeed, was as notable an
example of Virginia aristocratic enlightenment and distinction
as marked the early colonial epoch.

His secret diary for the years 1709-1712 was recently discovered, deciphered and published.[3] Its editors, who describe Mr.
Byrd as "Virginia's most polished and ornamental gentleman,"
state that he "felt that he was a kindly master and inveighed in
some of his letters against brutes who mistreat their slaves." We,
then, are not turning to an extreme when offering Mr. Byrd's

diary entries concerning his domestic slaves as indicating something of the realities behind the moonlight-and-magnolia fantasy.

2/8/09:   Jenny and Eugene were whipped.
4/17/09:   Anaka was whipped.
5/13/09:   Mrs. Byrd whips the nurse.
5/23/09:   Moll was whipped.
6/10/09:   "Eugene was whipped for running away and had the bit put on him." [This Eugene was a mere child.]
9/3/09:   "I beat Jenny . . ."
9/16/09:   Jenny was whipped.
9/19/09:   "I beat Anama . . ."
11/30/09:   Eugene and Jenny were whipped.
12/16/09:   "Eugene was whipped for doing nothing yesterday."

(In April Mr. Byrd was occupied in his official capacity in assisting the investigation of slaves "arraigned for high treason"—two were hanged.)

7/1/10:   "The Negro woman ran away again with the bit on her mouth."
7/8/10:   "The Negro woman was found and tied but ran away again in the night."
7/15/10:   Byrd reports the above woman caught and also adds of another slave: "My wife against my will caused little Jenny to be burned with a hot iron . . ."
7/19/10:   The same Negro woman again flees, but is retaken.
8/10/10:   Byrd reports the retaking of "my Negro girl" who had been a fugitive for three weeks.
8/22/10:   "I had a severe quarrel with little Jenny and beat her too much for which I was sorry."
8/31/10:   Eugene and Jenny beaten.
10/8/10:   Byrd whips three slave women.
11/6/10:   "The Negro woman ran away again."
11/13/10:   The Negro woman fugitive was found—dead.
1/11/11:   "I quarreled with my wife for being cruel to Brayne . . ."
1/22/11:   A slave "pretends to be sick." "I put a branding-iron on the place he complained of and put the bit on him."

2/2/11:	"My wife and little Jenny had a great quarrel in which my wife got the worst but at last by the help of the family Jenny was overcome and soundly whipped."
3/20/11:	He beats a Negro woman.
4/30/11:	He has two male slaves beaten.
5/1/11:	"I caused Prue to be whipped severely . . ."
8/4/11:	"I was indisposed with beating of Prue, and tired . . ."
9/26/11:	"I had several people whipped . . ."
9/28/11:	Eugene was whipped.
12/13/11:	His wife whips a slave while a guest is present. Byrd disapproves.
1/10/12:	A slave "pretends" he fell and hurt himself; he is forced to wear the bit for 24 hours.
2/5/12:	His wife causes several slaves to be whipped.
3/2/12:	His wife beats Jenny "with the tongs"; Byrd disapproves.
3/3/12:	Billy is beaten.
3/15/12:	Peter again claims to be ill and the bit is put in his mouth once more.
4/9/12:	His wife causes Molly to be whipped.
5/22/12:	His wife beats Prue very violently; he whips Anama severely.
6/6/12:	". . . found Prue with a candle by daylight, for which I gave her a salute with my foot."
6/30/12:	Three women and one man are beaten.
7/25/12:	Billy is whipped.
7/30/12:	Molly and Jenny whipped.
8/21/12:	Billy beaten.
9/3/12:	We come to the close of the volume and find that his wife "gave Prue a great whipping."

This, let it be repeated, was the household of colonial Virginia's "most polished and ornamental gentleman."

Against their enslavement the Negro people reacted everywhere—in Africa, aboard ship, in the West Indies and South America, and in the colonies that were to become the United States—with a determination to survive, a will to resist and a persistent militancy.

The modes of resistance, both individual and collective, were intensely varied. These included slowdown in work, shamming

illness, breaking tools, maltreating work animals, flight, arson,
attempts at assassination (especially with poison), self-mutilation
and destruction, infanticide, purchasing freedom, insurrection.
Above all, perhaps, it included the less dramatic but no less difficult faculty of retaining hope, of wanting to live, of preserving
dignity, of passing on to cherished children (though the master
class owned their bodies) the dream and the vision of the Time
of Freedom.

In any slave society the high point of unrest and discontent is
reached in insurrection. Specifically in American Negro slavery
so complete was the machinery of control, so outnumbered were
the slaves (never over 20 per cent of the total population and
never quite 40 per cent of the Southern population) and so
virulent was the system of racism, that the possibility of successful slave rebellion never existed.[4] Yet, as a remarkable manifestation of the magnificent spark of discontent that can never be
quenched in the hearts of exploited humanity stands the record of
incessant plots and uprisings among the American Negro slaves.

Here no more shall be attempted than the merest chronicling
of certain of the outstanding events of this nature that occurred
during the colonial period. Slave plots of considerable scope disturbed Virginia and Maryland in the late 1680's; their discovery
resulted in the executions of several slaves. In 1709 and 1710
the same pattern was repeated, though this time Indian and
Negro slaves were involved together. In 1712 rebellious slaves
killed and wounded about 15 whites in New York City, wherefore 21 slaves were executed—"some were burnt, others hanged,
one broke on the wheele, and one hung alive in chains," reported
the Governor.

Colonial South Carolina (where the slaves did outnumber the
whites through most of the period) was continually beset by
concerted slave unrest. Notable instances were the uprisings and
plots of 1713, 1720 and, especially, those which recurred from
1737 through 1741. Widespread plots were crushed in Virginia
in 1722 and 1723. New York City was disturbed in 1740 by
evidences of collective efforts by slaves at poisoning the water

supply; the next year the city was absolutely panic-stricken by reports (very much exaggerated) of the intention on the part of the slaves (with some white confederates) of burning the town. Certain it is that many fires did suddenly hit various parts of the city, and it is also certain that four whites were executed, 13 slaves were burned alive, 18 were hanged, and 70 banished—*i.e.*, sold into the West Indies.

Slave disaffection to a notable degree reappeared in South Carolina in 1759 and 1760. In northern Virginia, in 1767, several overseers were killed by poisoning, with the result that many slaves were arrested, some executed, "after which their heads were cut off, and fixed on the chimnies of the court-house." In the early 1770's, unrest and rebellion were reported from the slaves of Georgia (where slavery had been established 20 years before), and the last year prior to the Declaration of Independence was marked by a widespread conspiracy in North Carolina.

The conspiracies and revolts were stimulated by periods of depression (which resulted in actual starvation conditions for many of the slaves and others among the colonial poor) and by wars—against Indians, the Spanish or the French. At times there was unity in the plots amongst slaves and free Negroes, Negro slaves and Indian, and even among whites (especially indentured servants) and slaves. But in these cases the bulk of the rebels consisted of Negro slaves; and most of the slave insurrections of the colonial period (and thereafter, until 1850) involved Negro slaves alone.

IV

While this turmoil existed among the slaves, all was far from placidity among the indentured servants, who, with the slaves, made up about one-third of the whole colonial population. These —voluntary and involuntary, apprentices, bound-out convicts, redemptioners—constituted a group of laborers whose condition of living was but little above that of the chattel slaves. Men, women and children were involved in this indentured servitude, the vast majority of them whites, though up to about 1670 a considerable proportion were Negroes.

As previously indicated, the term of indenture varied from two to 14 years and even (in rare cases) to life. Few urban workers were of this category, except for domestic workers; but a very large percentage of the workers producing grain, tobacco, naval stores, and lumber were under indenture.

During the period of servitude, the worker received no pay in wages—his compensation came in bed and board, in learning a trade and, usually, at the termination of his service, in some small cash reward, clothing, tools and, at times, a grant of land from the government. His hours and conditions of work were set by the master and the servant's duty was to obey and to work diligently. Punishment was at the master's discretion and included severe physical "correction," while flight from the master was punishable not only by beatings but also by a doubling or tripling of the length of indenture.

Friendship between Negro slave, and white and Negro indentured servants was common throughout the 17th century and far from unknown in the 18th. Joint flight by Negro and white is repeatedly reported, while united participation in uprisings and conspiracies occurred at times. Neither slave nor indentured servant was permitted to marry; yet cohabitation between Negro and white is frequently noted in the colonial records.[5] The deliberate planting and spreading of white supremacist doctrine and habit by the planters and the rich generally is observable in the colonial era, with assemblies passing laws forbidding fraternization, ministers preaching against it, and masters and employers frowning upon it. Important in this connection was the employers' practice of pitting one group of workers against another and using slave workers to push down the wages of those who were free.

In an age noted for savagery and in a country where sadism was institutionalized as regards the relationship with the Indian and the Negro peoples, it is to be expected that the treatment accorded to indentured servants by omnipotent masters, lusting for wealth, was abominable. As the researches of Abbot E. Smith, Richard B. Morris and others have shown, these unfree workers were frequently beaten, were branded, chained to their tasks, had salt rubbed in their wounds and generally received something of the kind of physical maltreatment that slaves endured throughout their lives. Indicative was the preamble to a Virginia Act of 1662 aimed at curbing some of the worst excesses:

> The barbarous usage of some servants by cruell masters being so much scandall & infamy to the country in generall that people who would willingly adventure themselves hither, are through fears thereof diverted, & by that means the supplies of particular men & the well seating of his majesties country very much obstructed.

The white indentured servant did have greater protection than the slave through the courts—at least once, in Maryland in 1657, a master was actually hanged for the wanton killing of a servant. Moreover, with the white servant, the particular malice and viciousness produced by racism were not present; and the master of the servant had to remember that the man he beat today would be free in the more or less close future.

There were a few cases, in the colonial period, of masters being tried for the particularly brutal murder of slaves, but in only one case, so far as this writer has discovered, was there any punishment at all. That occurred in New York in 1686, where a master was tried for having whipped a slave woman to death. He was acquitted though the jury said it thought he should have been more "sparing" since the woman was "unsound"; but the master was required to pay the court costs!

With the indentured servants, as with the slaves, and as is true of the exploited of all times and climes, oppression met with resistance. Flight, singly or in groups (and often with slaves) was very common among the indentured servants. Individual forcible acts of resistance also dot colonial records and newspapers. Thus, by 1644, the Connecticut rulers already were complaining that the indentured servants were "stubborn, refractory and dis-

contented." There are, also, contemporary references to work
stoppages among indentured servants.

A good example was the refusal of six indentured servants in
Calvert County, Maryland, in 1663, to continue working for
their master. They complained that his supply of food was insufficient, and that they had been given no meat at all. Brought
into court, they were ordered to receive 30 lashes each and to
return to work. The servants, "kneeling, asking and craving for-
giveness," were favored with remission of the sentence, and released, though warned by the court "to be of good behavior of
their master hereafter." Conspiracy and rebellion, too, were not
uncommon; in addition, there was frequently mass participation
by indentured servants (much more often than slaves, for obvious reasons) in uprisings led by the free segments of the population against tyrannical landlords, eastern Nabobs, colonial proprietors or royal governors.

The conspiracies of the indentured ones occurred mainly in
the 17th century.[6] Particularly serious, for example, were the uprisings of the servants in parts of Virginia in 1661, 1663 (with
some slaves), and in 1681. In all cases the efforts for freedom
were brutally crushed and the leaders executed. The demands
were for less abominable conditions and better food, and at times
for complete freedom, as in the plot of 1661 in York County,
Virginia, led by Isaac Friend and William Clutton. At their trial
it was brought out that Friend had urged:

> that they would get a matter of forty of them together and
> get guns and he would be the first and lead them and cry as
> they went along *who would be for liberty and freed from bond-*
> *age* and that there would be enough come to them and they
> would go through the country and kill those that made any
> opposition and that they would either be free or die for it.

With the indentured servants, however, as with the slaves, the
single most common form of resistance to enforced labor was that
of flight. The contemporaneous evidence makes clear that this
represented a very real problem to the employers, and newspaper
advertisements for runaway servants are exceedingly common

prior to the Revolution. A fairly characteristic example appeared in the *Pennsylvania Gazette,* Sept. 8, 1773:

> Run away from the subscriber, living in Upper Penn's Neck, Salem County, on the 27th day of August last, a Scotch servant man, named James Dick, about 30 years of age, about 5 feet 8 inches, of a sandy complexion, with a fresh colour, down look and talks coarse; had on, when he went away, an iron collar (this being the eighth time he ran away) a dark beerskin jacket . . . whoever takes up the said servant, and secures him, so that his master may get him again, shall have three dollars reward, paid by Thomas Carey, junior.

Chapter IV

Class Conflict at Home: The Free

AMONG THE FREE laboring masses
of the American colonies, life was hard and militancy was widespread. As has already been indicated, for the 70 per cent of the colonial working population that was free, living conditions were better than for their class brothers in Europe and the degree of social mobility was somewhat higher, but each was true in a relative sense only. In an absolute sense, life was very onerous, for earnings were barely enough to put the plainest food into the mouths of the producer, his wife and his children, and in times of acute depression unemployment was rife and hunger was widespread. Social mobility existed, but for the vast majority of the free workers and poorer farmers status was fixed for life and was generally inherited by their children—moreover, the mobility worked both ways, up and down.

In the cities prostitution was rife, beggars abounded, poorhouses were crowded,[1] slums were already present, and the hundreds who depended on public relief to keep alive had to wear a badge reflecting their "degraded" status. In the rural areas the plainest fare, the rudest shelter, the coarsest clothing was the rule for almost all who labored with their own hands. And in cities and in farms the free poor worked as the poor have always worked—very hard and very long.

50

The rich lived in colonial America as they have lived everywhere. A town and country house; hundreds and thousands of acres; dozens of servants and/or slaves; lavish meals; incessant parties; silks and satins, velvets and pearls; carriages and gold plate; fashionable plays and music and books; affairs, alliances, intrigues; high and mighty offices; and intense pre-occupation with holding on to all this and rationalizing it, and keeping the "lower sort" in their proper place.

These differences were the work and the will of God, else they would not exist. He who questions them displays thereby his lack of faith and belief; he who questions them is of the devil and should be dealt with accordingly. The poor must be made to work and it is the fear of starving that will make them work. As for the beggars and idle fellows, true it is, wrote the Reverend Cotton Mather in 1695 (*Durable Riches*), they "shamefully grow upon us, and such beggars too as our Lord Jesus Christ hath expressly forbidden us to countenance." Hence, his apostolic advice: "Let them starve."

I

Class struggles among the colonial free manifested themselves on many levels and in many different ways. Ideologically the challenges to the oppressive status quo ran the gamut from attacks upon particular privileges to anarchistic and levelling proposals. Politically, proposals ranged from modifications of certain tax policies to the severing of all connections with Great Britain and the establishment of an egalitarian republic. Organizationally, activities included the strike of fishermen and the forcible ousting of a Royal governor.

Let us consider first, briefly, the urban poor and middling groups—the so-called common laborers, and the more skilled, like the seamen, artisans, mechanics, small tradesmen and craftsmen, who, with the slaves and indentured servants, made up by far the bulk of the city populations.

Here one finds in the midst of exhausting work, a kind of

seething unrest which continually breaks out into more or less dramatic episodes. Most of these people were illiterate and in any case they were without a press of their own. The chroniclers of colonial days, as of almost all history, were of the well-to-do and what records remain are largely those that these chroniclers produced. Despite these limitations, the picture of colonial life, as lived by the masses and as presented in available records, is one of deep unease and incessant striving for something better.

Professor Bridenbaugh, writing of urban colonial life, reports that "the workman was at the mercy of his employer, with no re-course and no guarantee against wage cuts or unemployment," and repeatedly from every city, came disturbing reports about "the poor People, many of whom are almost starving for want of employment." Yet, despite the fact of a complete absence of any legal protection and the naked favoring of the interests of the employer, and despite the competition offered by unfree labor, there are records of organized struggles by these colonial Ameri-can workers—of course, not like modern industrial workers—that anticipate later trade union battles.

Perhaps the earliest of the journeymen strikes (as contrasted with strikes by master craftsmen, which really were protests against governmental-regulated price levels) was that of fisher-men off the present Maine coast in 1636 for an advance in pay. There is record, too, of shipwrights in Gloucester, Massachusetts, being locked out by their employers in 1643. Fifteen out of 20 carters employed by New York City struck against low wages early in 1684. The city discharged the strikers from its employ, hired others and thus succeeded, in one week, in forcing the cart-men to appeal for re-employment. Only three of the men were reinstated, after being compelled to pay a fine of six shillings.

In the 18th century there are more frequent records of "labor troubles," though once again it is likely that only part of this story ever was recorded. One of the very earliest examples of organizational activity among domestic workers comes from New York City early in 1734. These women felt themselves sufficiently united to insert a notice in the city press of that time declaring:

> We think it reasonable we should not be beat by our Mistresses' husbands, they being too strong, and perhaps may do tender Women mischief. If any Ladies want Servants and will engage for their husbands, they will soon be supplied.

Some examples of a similar nature are reported during the 1740's. High wheat prices in New York City, caused in part by efforts at "cornering" the market by unscrupulous merchants, led the bakers in 1741 to announce that they collectively had agreed to produce no more bread until the price fell. In the same year, caulkers (workers who made ships water-tight) in Boston struck work in a demand that they be paid in money and not in notes negotiable in particular shops. In both these cases the results are not clear.

Labor activity among Southern workers was by no means unknown during the colonial period (and later). Thus, there is record of a strike for higher pay among the carpenters of Savannah as early as 1746, and the quite remarkable fact that Negro chimney sweepers (a craft largely confined to Negro workers) in Charleston in 1763 had formed "a combination amongst themselves, to raise the usual prices and to refuse doing their work," unless their demands were granted. Again, the results of this effort are not known; ominous, however, is the fact that the contemporary newspaper reporting the event, went on to comment, "Surely these are evils that require some attention to suppress."

Towards the end of the colonial period, in 1768, occurred a labor stoppage very closely resembling modern strikes. This involved about 20 journeymen tailors of New York City who refused to accept a reduction in wages ordered by the master tailors, pooled their resources and talents and opened up their own tailoring establishment—a very early example of a labor collective.

In addition, during periods of acute economic distress in the colonial cities, there were occasional desperate outbreaks by the famished, as happened in the so-called "bread-riots" in Boston in 1709 and 1713. Other causes sometimes resulted in outbreaks creating serious police problems for the authorities.

Thus, again in Boston, in 1747, a British naval officer finding himself short of crews, dispatched a press gang into the city and simply carried off several men—a practice which the colonists understood had been outlawed a generation earlier so far as their part of the world was concerned. Such press gangs selected their victims from the very poor, and this time that class responded with vigor. Many of them—Negro and white—assembled and agreed to remedy the situation in their own way. They seized several British naval officers strolling about the city and held them as hostages pending the release of the impressed Bostonians. They put a deputy sheriff in the stocks and surrounded the General Court, seeking redress. The Royal Governor, having vainly sought to talk the crowd into dispersing and giving up their hostages, called upon the militia to attack them; but he was alarmed to discover that the militia—made up of local men—was very slow to respond.

The Governor, terrified, retired to his castle and urged the British naval commander to release the impressed Bostonians. That officer responded by offering to put down the "rebellion" with the marines and naval men of his squadron. The town masses, on the other hand, showed no evidence of turning back from their course, insisted on retaining their hostages and began to wonder, audibly, if the governor had not actually abdicated his authority.

At this critical juncture, the town government itself took a stand against the masses and for "law and order," and assured the Governor of its respect, meanwhile denouncing their fellow townsmen as "Negroes and persons of vile condition."

The matter was settled when the British officer did free nearly all of those he had impressed, whereupon the hostages were likewise released, and the naval squadron left the port of Boston. Despite the support of the town's "respectability," Governor Shirley informed his superiors in London that the tumultuous behavior was the result of the town meetings that were so influential and of the generally "mobbish" and democratic atmosphere in the city.[2]

II

In the rural areas throughout the colonial period there were frequent dramatic manifestations of intense class struggle between the rich and the poor (other than the unfree). At the moment I do not have in mind those revolts and uprisings which were multi-class in nature, though usually in them the poor made up a majority of the rebels—as that led by Bacon in Virginia or by Leisler in New York. Movements of this nature will be discussed hereafter, but there were, additionally, during the colonial period, organized stirrings which seem to have been confined pretty much to the rural poor.

An example of this kind of activity was the so-called "tobacco-cutting riots" in Virginia in 1682. Hard times afflicted the colonists, with bare necessities being difficult to come by. A mark of the economic depression was the fact that tobacco had fallen to a penny a pound, so that its production was profitless. Colonial efforts at building up manufactures and tiade were crushed by the English government; there seemed nowhere to turn and conditions grew increasingly bad. An effort was started to limit the production of tobacco in the hope of stimulating its price and also inducing a more diversified economy. This too was blocked by the English rulers; finally, groups of colonists went from plantation to plantation destroying the tobacco crop. Contemporaries declared that only "inconsiderable people" were so bold as to do this. The military crushed their flouting of "good order" and two of the leaders were executed.

Throughout the 18th century, in colony after colony, there were uprisings of debtor farmers aimed at eliminating feudal burdens (particularly in the Hudson River valley region of New York), throwing off heavy taxes, limiting the political power of the planters, merchants and creditors of the East, and reversing a steady tight-money, deflationary policy that favored creditors at the expense of debtors. Of these agrarian conflicts the most wide-spread and prolonged occurred in the colonies of New York, New Jersey and North Carolina.

The New York difficulties—definitively analyzed in the work of Irving Mark—span practically the entire 18th century up to the Revolution, and as a matter of fact break out with renewed fierceness in the middle of the next century, too. Beginning with 1711, there was hardly a year that mass agrarian disturbances of some kind did not occur in that colony, the culminating explosion coming in a general uprising of the Hudson River valley farmers in 1766.

The essence of the unrest lay in the fact that by 1697—through graft, favoritism and speculation—four families, the Van Cortlandts, Philipses, Livingstons and Van Rensselaers, had become the owners of over 1,600,000 acres of land, comprising much of the present counties of Westchester, Dutchess, Albany, Putnam, Columbia and Rensselaer. These landlords, avaricious at best, were especially intolerable because they possessed patroonships, or, in effect, feudal manors, so that those farming the land could never hope to own it or the improvements upon it and were also directly subordinate, in court procedure and political representation, to the great landowners.

The widespread uprising of 1766 on the part of the New York peasants—a term contemporaneously used—was undoubtedly stimulated by the militancy displayed by workers, artisans and mechanics in the Sons of Liberty within New York City. British officials saw the two as really one threat so that Sir Henry Seymour Conway, of the Cabinet, instructed Governor Moore of New York in October, 1765, to use "the utmost exertion of your prudence . . . and the vigour necessary to suppress outrage and violence [of] the lower and more ignorant of the people."

Urban and rural unity, however, was not established—though some degree of real sympathy did exist—and the apparatus of the rich, with the assistance of the force supplied by the British Crown, was able to crush the destitute farmers.

Those farmers had tried year after year to obtain some semblance of justice from the courts or some indication of reform from the provincial government, but both were sheer instrumentalities of their oppressors. As one of their chief leaders, William Prendergast, put it, the tenant farmers "could not be defended in a Court of Law because they were poor; therefore they were determined to do themselves justice; poor men were always oppressed by the rich." Armed combat followed; the landlords finding the militia unreliable, the actual suppression fell to regular British troops.

About 80 of the rebels were arrested and were variously punished with pillory, fine, or imprisonment. Prendergast was sentenced to be hanged and quartered, but the sheriff was unable to find any one to execute the gruesome sentence. After several months in prison, and helped very much by the exceptionally energetic defense efforts of his wife, the Governor recommended to the King—bearing in mind Prendergast's great popularity—that he be pardoned. After a further delay this was done by the King.

Militant unrest on the part of the rural masses was also characteristic of New Jersey throughout the 1740's and up to at least 1754. Here the rulers' efforts at suppression were complicated not only by the normal unreliability of the local militia, but also by an actual mutiny of New Jersey troops in 1740.

Excessive rents, economic depression, the existence of feudal taxes such as quit rents, political deprivation, and the wholesale fraud of the rich, motivated the Jersey farmers, especially in the eastern section of the colony, in their defiance of court orders, breaking up of sheriffs' sales, and efforts to rescue their brothers from jail. Their uprisings were finally crushed, but at least one demand, the termination of the collection of quit rents, was won by this militant action in New Jersey.

Similar grievances motivated the poorer farmers of North Carolina—in the counties west of Tidewater—to organize themselves collectively under the title of Regulators and to try to get some political and economic relief.

By 1764, the majority of the farmers in Anson, Halifax, Orange, and Granville counties were organied; they demanded a more equitable tax system, an end to extortionate fees, and an accounting by the sheriffs of the taxes they collected. The demands being rejected, sporadic outbreaks occurred throughout the 1760's. Finally, in 1771, the Royal Governor, Tryon,[3] marched into Regulator territory at the head of a force top-heavy with officers (many of the privates balked at fighting) and at the Battle of Alamance, near Hillsborough, inflicted heavy casualties upon the Regulators. Large numbers were jailed and seven were hanged; others submitted, and still others fled westward as political refugees. These last, led by James Robertson, made the first permanent non-Indian settlements in what is today Tennessee.

Chapter V

Multi-Class Outbreaks

WITHIN THE CLASS-STRATIFIED colonial society, as has been demonstrated, each of the classes conducted its own individual struggles—or campaigns of repression—with only occasional combining of forces, as when indentured servants and slaves battled together, or the poor of the cities and farms gave each other assistance. But the fact is that all these cases—of slaves and indentured servants, of debtor farmers and patroon-bound peasants, of laborers, artisans, and mechanics—represented basically separate and distinct efforts.

In addition, throughout the colonial era, the antagonisms and contradictions of the social order manifested themselves in uprisings and rebellions that were multi-class in nature, with certain merchants and planters leading other classes—mechanics, urban petty-bourgeoisie, debtor farmers, indentured servants, and (rarely) slaves—in more or less combined array against officials representing either the Proprietors or the Crown directly. These outbreaks were high points in a social unrest that more commonly manifested itself in the expression of ideas, the advancing of proposals, the development of political platforms, and the crystallizing of oppositional groups. All these, in turn, were products of the fundamental and growing divergences between the English rulers and the American colonists.

It is a striking fact that multi-class outbreaks were concentrated almost entirely in the 17th century, and were rare in the next one until the grand and successful explosion known as *the*

American Revolution. In the earlier century the marked insta-
bility in English politics—with its two revolutions—had a major
impact in promoting or encouraging similar events on a smaller
scale in the colonies.[1] Moreover, the general rawness of English
colonial administration in that first century of its existence induced frequent resort to violence by the colonists. In the 17th
century, also, there were very much fewer legitimate political
and legislative means open to the colonists for the expression and
the working out of their grievances than there were to be, especially for the more affluential amongst them, a century later and
this made the earlier time a more violent one in its general political nature.

We turn now to a brief chronicle of the more important general uprisings marking the colonial epoch.

I

One of the earliest, back in 1635 in Virginia (when the colony
did not have over 7,000 inhabitants), is of consequence because
it demonstrates a dominant strand in all these conflicts, namely,
a tendency on the part of the colonial legislature to curb the
authority of Royal (or Proprietary) governors and to enhance
its own. The details of this event are too complex to require full
elucidation in this work: The point is that a lucrative trading
post set up in Kent Island, between Maryland and Virginia, by
one William Claiborne and his associates, became an object of
acrimonious debate between the authorities of the two colonies.
Claiborne, backed by the Virginia House of Burgesses (in which
actually sat a representative from Kent Island), refused to honor
the Maryland Proprietor's demand that he trade from the Island only with a license granted by that Proprietor. Virginia's
Governor, John Harvey, sided with the Proprietor, removed
Claiborne from his office as Secretary of Virginia and jailed another official who sympathized with Claiborne. This sparked a
revolt, led by a former indentured servant, Samuel Mathews

(elected Governor by the Council some 30 years later) and involving several hundred armed men, which resulted in the removal of the obnoxious Governor.

It was the Maryland Proprietor's turn next. With the beginning of the Civil War in England, in 1642 (the King flees in 1646; Cromwell beheads him in 1649) one finds its contest transplanted to Maryland, with special intensity because of the Catholic faith of its Proprietor. Portentous was the arrest in 1644 by the Maryland Governor of the Protestant Captain, Richard Ingle, master of a trading vessel appropriately named the *Reformation*. This, coupled with the news that the Proprietor planned to intercede on the side of the King in the War, led to the overthrow of the Proprietor and his flight to Virginia where the Royal Governor, Sir William Berkeley, gave him refuge. For two years Maryland was locally governed, the Proprietor not being returned until 1647.

There followed a period of concessions and reforms on the part of Lord Baltimore, including some liberalizing of the colonial assembly, the appointment of a Protestant Governor, William Stone, the welcoming of Puritans to Maryland, and the issuance, in 1649, of the justly-famed Toleration Act. This last protected freedom of "conscience in matters of religion," for those accepting Christ's divinity, and specifically outlawed deprecatory references to "heretick, Scismatick, Idolator, puritan, Independant, Presbiterian, popish prest, Jesuite, Lutheran, Calenist, Anabaptist, Brownist, Antinomian, Barrowist, Roundhead, Sepatist, or any other."

Yet there was hesitancy on the part of the Proprietor to acknowledge subordination to the Protectorate in England. This, combined with popular unrest induced by increasing concentration of land ownership, the continued domination of the Lord Proprietor, the latter's insistence on collecting quit-rents, and economic depression, resulted in the Proprietor's party losing control altogether of the provincial assembly. The Governor sought by arms to defeat the anti-Proprietor's party, but was overcome in battle in March, 1655. Here, himself wounded, the Governor was jailed, four of his followers were executed and for three years Maryland once again was locally governed.

Again the restoration of the Proprietor in 1657 proved temporary, because his governor, Josias Fendall, allied himself with the popular majority in the assembly. In 1660, Maryland announced itself a republic, with Fendall probably aiming at uniting some of the other colonies under a system mimicking that of, and subordinate to, Cromwell in England.[2] But that very year Charles II was restored to his father's throne. Fendall was removed and condemned (and barred from holding office in the future, but is heard of again, nevertheless) and the Proprietor was restored.

II

Elsewhere opposition to Proprietary rule, land engrossment, and quit-rent payments also burst forth in organized revolt. An instance is that of New Jersey in 1670, whose inhabitants rebelled, stopped quit-rent payments, established their own "rump" assembly and held control until the Dutch reconquest of New York and New Jersey in 1673. This in turn was undone, with the colonies being returned to the English by the Treaty of Westminster in 1674—who promptly restored the situation prevailing in New Jersey prior to the "upstart riots" of 1670.

But, the outstanding example of popular uprising, prior to the American Revolution itself, is Bacon's Rebellion of 1676. Concerning this there is a large body of published material, most notably the work of Thomas Jefferson Wertenbaker, and here but the barest summary is necessary.

Bacon's Rebellion was a harbinger of the greater rebellion that was to follow it by exactly a century. The Virginia uprising was directed against the economic subordination and exploitation of the colony by the English rulers, and against the tyrannical and corrupt administrative practices in the colony which were instituted for the purpose of enforcing that subordination. Hence, the effort led by the young planter, Nathaniel Bacon, was multi-class, encompassing in its ranks slaves, indentured servants, free farmers and many planters; it was one in which women were, as an anti-Baconite contemporary noted, "great encouragers and assisters"; and it was one in which demands for political reform along democratic lines formed a central feature of the movement.

Specifically, Virginians found themselves caught in a vise of economic strangulation and political domination from which nothing promised relief but an appeal to arms. The Navigation Acts, passed in 1660, by giving the British a monopoly of the tobacco crop, had resulted in the fall of tobacco within a few years from three pence a pound, to less than half a penny. At the same time, the identical enactments had confined the Virginia market (and Maryland and North Carolina—then called Albemarle County) to the British merchants who, without competition, raised the prices on finished goods.

The scissors—the gap between what tobacco sold for and what purchased goods cost—expanding, Virginia planters and farmers went heavily in debt to British merchants, in the hope that loans would see them through the economic difficulties. But with the loans, went exorbitant interest charges which meant additional burdens rather than relief, and tighter dependence upon the British.

Efforts on the part of the colonists to meet the situation through diversifying their crops, or through industrial or commercial ventures resulted in effective negatives from England. And efforts to avoid the full impact of England's monopoly over the purchase of the tobacco crop by developing a strong inter-colonial trade in tobacco led to an Act, in 1673, placing a prohibitive tax of one penny a pound on tobacco shipped from one province to another.

These measures hit all planters, but they hit hardest at those with least wealth, for the richest had lower per-unit cost of production (especially through the use of slave labor, which became of some consequence by the early 1670's along the eastern seaboard) and could get better borrowing terms. Moreover, the wealthy were able to invest in merchandising and in fur trading when tobacco planting was especially unprofitable.

Special circumstances aggravated the already very bad conditions. Of these three were of great consequence. One was the Anglo-Dutch rivalry (a prime source of the Navigation Acts, in the first place) which led to three wars, the last two of them fought 1664-1667 and 1672-1673. These resulted in very great loss to planters through the capture or destruction of merchant ships carrying tobacco and other crops. Second, a devastating hurricane, in 1667, left thousands homeless and destroyed most of the tobacco crop; and third, in 1672-73, an epidemic destroyed half the cattle in Virginia.

Added to this were colonial and county tax systems which discriminated against the moderately well-off and the poor and sharply in favor of the greatest landowners, and which kept getting more and more burdensome as the years went by. Thus, when taxes were raised yet again in 1674, scores of farmers gathered, arms in hand, in Kent County and swore to prevent their collection. Only upon the Royal Governor Berkeley's warning that those who persisted in their defiance would meet the fate of traitors, did the men disperse—to gather in greater force and throughout the colony after two more years of exasperation and after the appearance of a leader.

Nor does this yet explain, fully, the resort to arms in 1676. An additional strong cause was the perversion of the governmental apparatus by the Royal Governor and his class brothers who dominated the Council. Berkeley succeeded in building up a powerful political machine and thereby taking over control of the House of Burgesses, so that that (relatively) "popular" branch of colonial government, filled with Berkelian placemen, sat continuously, without fresh elections, from 1661, until imminent revolution forced Berkeley to call for an election early in 1676. And, by an act of 1670, the franchise was taken from all who were not landowners.

Meanwhile, through their wealth and their influence in London and their control of the colonial governmental apparatus, including the courts, Berkeley and his cohorts lived in startling luxury, granted themselves the choicest lands, took the most lucrative public offices, pocketed much of the taxes, and won a monopoly of the extremely profitable fur trade.

So it was that Bacon, newly-come to Virginia, the descendant of nobility (he was kin to Francis Bacon) and himself a tobacco planter in the Virginia frontier region, was moved to declare, in 1675: "The poverty of the Country is such that all the power and sway is got into the hands of the rich, who by extortious advantages, having the common people in their debt, have always curbed and oppressed them in all manner of ways." And further, that how to mend matters was a great puzzlement since appeal had to be made to "the very persons our complaints do accuse."

Indian difficulties formed the catalyst of rebellion. These, of course, had begun with the colony's beginnings. Peace of a sort had come with a treaty of 1646, in which certain lands of Virginia were set aside for the use of the colonizers and the Indians respectively. Within two years the English had broken the agreement in fact, and broke it in law by 1649. There followed intense English expansion into Indian lands and so vigorous a practice of the indiscriminate killing of Indians that even the Virginia legislature tried to call a halt, in 1656, noting its "sad apprehension of the small account . . . of late made of shedding Indians' blood, though never so innocent." An Act passed six years later likewise admitted that growing Indian hostility was due to "violent intrusions of diverse English made into their [the Indians'] lands."

Matters with the Indians came to a head in 1675 when Virginians joined with Marylanders in a campaign of extermination aimed at the Susquehannas. At one point, some chiefs sent out as a truce party were treacherously seized by Virginians under a Major Trueman and slaughtered. As a result more or less sporadic warfare broke out all along the Virginia frontier, and the cry went up for governmental armed assistance.

This was slow in coming though certainly not because of any tenderness on the part of the Berkeley group. It was slow in coming for that group made thousands of pounds from the Indian trade—buying fur and selling them many things in exchange—including guns, the westerners always believed. Hence, Bacon's remark: "These traders at the head of the rivers buy and sell our blood."

This was the precipitant of Bacon's treason. He organized and led an expedition against the Indians, without the Governor's permission, and for this was denounced a traitor. Nevertheless, Bacon's popularity was so great (he was elected to the House of Burgesses, though tainted a traitor, in the elections of 1676 that Berkeley finally called to assuage public ill-will) and the people's suffering so intense, that the traitor ousted the Governor. The details of the actual conflict between the Baconians and the forces of the Royal Governor need not be gone into here; suffice it to say that in pitched battle the Baconians won and drove the Governor from the capital and gained control of the colony for several months in 1676.

It is clear that Bacon envisaged a united resistance to colonial oppressions on the part of North Carolina, Maryland and Virginia; it is even probable that he desired to create this unity for the purpose of breaking away from England completely, which seems, also, to have been the dream somewhat earlier of Josias Fendall. Indeed, Professor Wertenbaker believes that had the Bacon insurrection occurred a few years earlier—during the Third Anglo-Dutch War—"it is possible that the entire Chesapeake Bay region might have been lost to England."

But such unity was not forged, though some efforts were made; and England was not then occupied in wars. Bacon's attempt failed. He himself, not yet thirty and, as a contemporary said, "the hopes and Darling of the People," died of a fever in August, 1676, and though fighting continued thereafter, Berkeley was back in full control early in 1677. Now, supported by 1,100 British troops, sent for the purpose, the Governor restored "order."

In the course of accomplishing this, 37 of the leading Baconians were executed. Most died without their executioners recording what they might have said, but record does exist of what one of them, Anthony Arnold, told the Royal Judges. "Kings have no rights," he said, "but what they got by conquest and the sword, and he who can by force of the sword deprive them thereof has as good and just a title to them as the King himself. If the King should deny to do me right I would think no more of it to sheath my sword in his heart or bowels than of my mortal enemies." Anthony Arnold, "resolved rebel and traitor," was given a special execution. He was removed to his own immediate neighborhood and there hanged in chains, "to be a more remarkable example than the rest."

The Commissioners sent by the King to look into the Virginia troubles soon realized that if the vengeful Berkeley were left to his purposes England might well lose Virginia. Berkeley was returned to England (where he very soon died) and another Governor replaced him. Certain reforms adopted by the "Bacon Legislature" were retained, including those which extended the suffrage to all free men (including free Negroes, who voted in Virginia until 1723), the powers of the Council were curtailed, county government was somewhat democratized, and greater popular control was provided in the enactment and collecting of taxes. Rather sweeping amnesties were also promulgated.

But no fundamental changes were made; on the contrary the supremacy of the English Parliament was affirmed, the Navigation Acts remained in force and, in a word, Virginia remained a colony. To end that, revolution, not reform was required.[3]

III

Bacon's hopes for unity with Maryland and with Albemarle (North Carolina) sprang from the fact that the other two colonies suffered even as did Virginia from the Navigation Acts, from the tax act of 1673, from low-priced tobacco and from the deprivation of political and judicial rights. The fact is that in both of them there were uprisings—on modest scales, compared with Bacon's—though in these cases they were directed against Proprietors rather than a Royal Governor.

In September, 1676, some 60 persons, led by William Davyes and John Pate, gathered in Calvert County, Maryland, and announced their opposition to current taxation and franchise policies and their intention not to swear to a loyalty oath newly demanded by the (Catholic) Proprietor. The meeting was forcibly dispersed, its objects denounced as treasonous, and Davyes and Pate were hanged.

Other leaders of the protest movement stepped forward, especially Josias Fendall again, and John Coode, and the Maryland authorities promised suffrage and taxation reforms. The failure to implement these promises led to another minor uprising, in 1681, which was suppressed; but a greater one, in 1689, again led by Coode, was to have more success.

Also in 1676, under the leadership of George Durant and John Culpeper, organized resistance appeared in Albemarle to efforts by the Proprietor's agent, Thomas Miller, to enforce the payment of quit-rent and certain tobacco taxes. Here the opposition was powerful enough to force the release from jail of Durant and the recall of the obnoxious Miller, but in neither Maryland nor in Albemarle, even as in Virginia, were truly significant alterations in the colonial apparatus obtained.

IV

The grievances of all the colonies overflowed the dam formed by Royal repression, with the "Glorious Revolution" in England. The impact of that event was tremendous throughout the colonial world and led to revolutionary attempts, collectively participated in by diverse classes in colonial society, notably in New England, New York, Maryland and North Carolina.

New England heard of the overthrow of James II in March, 1689. By the middle of April an uprising occurred in Boston, little blood was shed, Governor Andros and certain of his chief officers were arrested, and each of the New England colonies re-adopted its separate political existence as it had existed prior to the Restoration of the Stuarts.

In New York the arbitrary government dominated by the great landlords and merchants—Bayard, Van Cortlandt, and Schuyler—who had run affairs very much like a closed corporation and had in the course of this aroused deep opposition among the entire remaining population, faced rebellion under the leadership of Jacob Leisler. After a brief skirmish between the mutinous militia and a few dispirited regular British troops, the latter caved in, and the acting governor, Nicholson, sailed back to England. From 1689 to 1691 most of New York was ruled by the Leisler revolutionary government representing a coalition of the smaller merchants, the storekeepers, artisans and mechanics. Under this government certain landed and commercial monopolies were dissolved, advances in self-government were made, and reforms instituted in the tax system.

Meanwhile, in England, though Leisler protested his loyalty to the newly-ascendant Protestant majesties, William himself refused to cherish such goings-on as the taking into their own hands, by the majority of New York City inhabitants, of their own government. The King appointed a Colonel Henry Sloughter, Governor of his New York province and sent him, with soldiers, to take over the post.

War with France delayed the departure of Sloughter for several months, and only a part of his expedition arrived in New York. This group, under a Captain Ingolsby, demanded the surrender of the city, but Leisler would not oblige, and after a minor skirmish, succeeded in restraining the Captain. Finally, early in 1691, Sloughter himself did arrive and placed Leisler and his son-in-law, Milborne, under arrest.

Leisler's opponents, Bayard, Nichols and Livingston, pressured the Governor into ordering the execution of Leisler and Milborne, and both were hanged before their appeal from the death sentence had even been heard by the Crown. Most of the democratic reforms of Leisler were undone, although the existence of an Assembly—unknown in New York before Leisler—was affirmed, albeit its powers were rather circumscribed. The Leisler wing in New York politics remained potent for years after his execution. In 1695, Parliament was prevailed upon to remove the attainder of treason from Jacob Leisler's name and to restore his estate to his heirs. Furthermore, the New York Assembly, in 1702, voted an indemnity of £2,700 to those heirs.

The "Glorious Revolution" in England helped stimulate revolutionary events in Maryland, too. That Proprietary government had been swept by unrest continually, as we have already seen. A characteristic reply to this by the ruler was a tightening of his control, so that, in 1670, it was decreed that the Governor himself would fix the number of representatives to be allowed to each county in the provincial government, and that none but that official could change this number.

The Proprietor, moreover, dealt with the colony as though it were indeed simply his property, rather than the habitation of several thousand families, so that he made of its offices mere sinecures for his relatives and personal friends. Heavy assessment and taxes and great corruption followed, and scandals recurred, as when the acting governor, George Talbot (Lord Baltimore's nephew) murdered the royal collector of customs and fled the colony.

It was this last act that led the Proprietor to appoint as his deputy, and the president of the colony's Council, one William Joseph, an intense Jacobite in politics and a fervid Catholic. Greeting the provincial legislature late in 1688 he informed its members that, "There is no power but of God and the power by which we are assembled here is undoubtedly derived from God, to the King and from the King to his Excellency the Lord Proprietor and from his said Lordship to us." This was fine and classical doctrine for medieval Europe and for absolute monarchy, but rather anachronistic for late 17th century English political theorizing and certainly backward, not to say provocative, for late 17th century English America.

Shortly after Joseph had assured the colonial planters and

merchants that their sole duty was to obey his Lordship, the English bourgeoisie made good their rejection of such ideas with the crowning of William and Mary, and with the adoption of the Bill of Rights of 1689, in which the supremacy of Parliament was affirmed.

The Lord Proprietor was slow in directing his Maryland colony to acknowledge the overthrow of James, and the new order of things, and the Lord's officials in America were even slower in implementing such direction. When it appeared that these officials were fortifying the statehouse at St. Mary's, capital of the Province, several hundred men, led by the old rebel, John Coode, marched on the city and with almost no resistance—since the Governor's troops refused to fight—took over command. Shortly thereafter, August 1, 1689, Joseph himself surrendered, and the insurgents, under the name of the "Association in arms for the defense of the Protestant religion" (or, more simply, the Protestant Association), and in convention assembled, announced the ousting of the Lord Proprietor and their loyalty to the monarchs of the Revolution.

The Association then called the Assembly into session, and that body, which in November, 1688, had heard the Proprietor's officer assure them that they were without power, now in August, 1689, set up an interim government and sent Coode, the rebel, to England to get Royal confirmation of their acts. In 1691, Maryland passed out of the political control of the Proprietor (whose property rights, however, were not molested) and became a royal colony, with a governor, council and assembly.

It is worth noting that the revolutionary Coode government was in regular communication with the rebel government in New York and that both expressed a desire for cooperation and unity. This solidarity appeared, as we have seen, in earlier rebellions and reflected a growing sense of solidarity in the colonies generally.

V

In South Carolina and Albemarle County, popular unrest was at
a boiling point throughout the latter half of the 17th century.
Insurrectionary attempts were made in both areas consequent
upon the "Glorious Revolution," but in both the Proprietors
managed to hold on for another generation. In 1719, after severe
religious dissensions with the Proprietors, and after these worthies
had disallowed certain laws passed by the assembly, including one
regulating elections to that body—and contemporaneous with
severe economic depression, Indian attacks and threats of war
with Spain—revolution succeeded in Albemarle and in South
Carolina. Parliament in 1729 confirmed the ousting of the Proprietors and set up two separate royal colonies in North and
South Carolina.

Charles M. Andrews, whose monumental study, *The Colonial
Period of American History,* is of special value because of the
light it sheds on the facts concerning these uprisings against the
colonial Proprietors, evaluated them in a way with which this
writer cannot agree. Professor Andrews, in the second volume of
the aforementioned work, having in mind specifically the Maryland events, wrote:

> It is a mistake to read into such a protest anything demo-
> cratic or anything anticipatory of the American Revolution, for
> the agitation was for those rights enjoyed by Englishmen of the
> seventeenth century and nothing more. Such a system [as that
> of the Proprietors], absolute and paternal and demanding from
> all within its jurisdiction unqualified submission and obedience,
> provoked resistance, because it did not guarantee to the people
> of Maryland the rights of free-born Englishmen, such as the
> subjects of the king were then enjoying at home.

But is not the struggle for "the rights of free-born Englishmen"
by people living under a system demanding "unqualified submission and obedience," one which had democratic content,
when viewed historically, no matter how limited may have been
the rights of such Englishmen in the 17th century? And is not

the American Revolution conducted under the slogan of the demand for the rights of Englishmen? True it is that this is in another century, and the rights had in the meantime somewhat expanded; true it is also that the colonists in order to obtain the rights of Englishmen discovered during their Revolution that they had to cease being Englishmen. But is there nothing "anticipatory" at all in the fact that the colonists, separated by 90 years, do fight for an extension of their freedoms under the same slogan—and that these are the same colonies and the same colonial power?

The events of 1688-89 in England did further political and religious freedom in the colonies. The assertion of the supremacy of Parliament in the affairs of England bulwarked the claims of colonial legislatures for their supremacy in terms of colonial government, especially where such government was concerned with purely internal colonial affairs. The whole emphasis given to concepts of individual freedom, summed up in the term "the rights of Englishmen," became, too, precious to the colonists and of enormous consequence to their thinking and writing.

This concern for individual liberty and for self-government, or, at least, for the supremacy of the colonial legislatures in matters purely colonial, was to grow as the colonies themselves grew, and as their social orders matured. At the same time, the triumph of Parliament in England did not mean a lessening of concentration by the English bourgeoisie—now ensconced in power, albeit in alliance with the great landowners—on the subordination of the colonies and the use of them for the enrichment of that class and the enhancement of its power.

Chapter VI

Colonial Political Struggles

VIOLENT OUTBREAKS REPRESENTED, of course, highpoints in the class struggles which were the reality of colonial politics. This reality demonstrated itself most often in non-violent efforts, taking parliamentary, agitational and ideological forms where and when the possibilities for such expressions were present.

These struggles, as those which took violent form, revolved around basic questions of land ownership, taxation and money policies and the right to participate in government. They involved, fundamentally, an effort by the masses of people to enhance their political power and their conditions of living, and a response of repression to this effort by the dominant classes. At the same time, they impinged on the colonial relationship, because the popular surge for political and economic improvements invariably met, as an ultimate obstacle, the power of the English government. There is a partial exception to this in the colonial efforts to get rid of Proprietary overlordship—this, especially after 1689, coincided with a phase of British parliamentary policy. Involved here was a battle against feudal and neo-feudal forms towards which Parliament, too, was increasingly hostile; yet the fact is that the English government never rejoiced at *colonial initiative* in eliminating Proprietary power and often assisted the latter in fighting a delaying action.

Of the innumerable examples of political combat during the colonial era, three may be selected as especially noteworthy and as typifying several central features of its history. These are the Land Bank War of Massachusetts, the case of the Parson's Cause in Virginia, and the struggle around the writs of assistance, centering in Massachusetts.

I

To understand the events around the Massachusetts Land Bank it is necessary to bear in mind that a main feature of the colonies' subordination to the dominant English economic interests was the relationship between them as concerns the monetary system. England was intent on keeping her colonies bound to the pound, and to keep the currency of the colonies highly contracted. In this way the colonies could be more firmly held in financial dependence, their trade could be more effectively controlled, the direction of their economic development more easily guided, and the interests of British merchants and creditors better protected.

As a result, England forbade the exportation to the colonies of English coins; prohibited the colonies from restraining the exportation *from the colonies* of foreign coinage or of bullion; illegalized the establishment of colonial mints; and regularly discouraged the emissions of bills of credit within the colonies.

This monetary policy was, in fact, an important deterrent to the expansion of the colonial economy and to the building up of considerable fluid capital. Its severely deflationary effect consistently prejudiced the interests of debtors in particular. It resulted in the widespread use of commodities—as tobacco and grain—as in fact money, and in the development of several schemes for the expansion of colonial monetary exchange.

Among these were the so-called land banks, which were capitalized organizations, from which one could obtain bills of credit on the basis of land mortgages held by the banks. The idea was, then, to use these bills of credit (granted at rather low rates of interest, ranging from three to five per cent) as a substitute for money.

Schemes of this nature were always favored by rural and

urban debtors and condemned by the largest colonial merchants
and by the English capitalist community. These constituted the
creditors and so wanted interest and principal paid off in de-
flated—or at any rate, certainly not inflated—money.

This whole question of currency, involving as it did credit and
debts and the difference between prosperous economic activity
and choking stringency, foreclosure and bankruptcy, formed a
dominant note in colonial politics. In Massachusetts by 1740 the
country and city debtor classes, constituting the overwhelming
majority of the population, gained control of the provincial assembly and proceeded to establish a "Land & Manufacturers
Bank," which sought to loosen the currency and encourage colonial industry.

The Land Bank Party was at once denounced by the rich as
"the rabble" and "the Mobility." The Royal Governor, Jonathan
Belcher, issued instructions dismissing any officeholder who accepted Land Bank Bills of credit (whereupon Deacon Adams,
father of Samuel, Land Bank leader, and a Justice of Peace,
resigned his office and accused the Governor of acting against
"the interests of our native country.") But the Land Bank Party
continued to grow and the Governor feared it would sweep aside
all opposition in the pending elections of 1741. Hence, just prior
to those elections, the Governor announced the "discovery" of a
horrendous plot, whose details were left conveniently vague; but
armed with the announcement, the Governor imprisoned several
of the leaders of the Land Bank Party. Nevertheless, in the 1741
elections, that Party strengthened its grip on the legislature.

The result was that the British government came to the aid of
the merchants and the English creditors by outlawing the Land
Bank institution and declaring criminals those responsible for it.
The blow crippled the popular party for some years, and very
nearly precipitated revolution and civil war a generation ahead
of time; indeed, actual hostilities were only avoided by the English government's removal of Belcher and his replacement as
Governor by William Shirley.

In this case, the ruling class demonstrated its characteristic contempt for its own laws when those were embarrassing. Thus, the late James Truslow Adams, whose account is clearly biased in favor of the so-called "sound money" advocates, admits that their actions directed toward preventing the circulation of Land Bank notes, "were to a considerable extent extralegal." Moreover, the actual "legal" killing, by Parliament, of the Land Bank program was accomplished only by applying retroactively legislation passed 20 years earlier.

II

The conflict between debtor and creditor—extending of necessity into a battle with the English authorities—is dramatically illustrated, also, in the Parson's Cause of Virginia, which first introduced Patrick Henry to fame. That case arose out of the passage by the debtor-dominated Virginia legislature of an act in 1755 (repealed in 1758) which permitted the payment of taxes, rents, fees, contracts and debts—which for generations had been paid in the colony in tobacco—in money at the rate of two pence per pound of tobacco due.

This act was passed in the midst of war and after drought, catastrophes that had pushed the price of tobacco up to about 6 pence per pound; and it was passed, as the Assembly said, to prevent creditors "from taking advantage of the necessities of the people." It had all the more unanimity in Virginia since the planters as a class were perpetually and heavily in debt to British merchants, moving one of them, Thomas Jefferson, to complain that "these debts had become hereditary from father to son, for many generations, so that the planters were a species of property, annexed to certain mercantile houses in London."

The creditors decided to fight this legislation and to do it in the way politically most apt. They backed the efforts of the state-supported Anglican clergy to have the law declared invalid and to be paid—their salaries, for generations, had been set at 16,000 pounds of tobacco annually—in the current market price of tobacco.

On the petition of these clergy, and with the active support of the English mercantile interest, the Privy Council declared, in 1759, the Virginia act of the preceding year to be void and ordered payment in full, plus damages. But the Virginia House of Burgesses with Richard Bland in the lead, decided to contest the Council's (*i.e.,* the King's) ruling. In the struggle against the Council's veto, the House of Burgesses set up a committee of correspondence, to establish contact with an agent in England and to serve as a means of getting the colony's viewpoint out quickly—an historic precedent for the later committees of correspondence.

The decisive case was heard, November-December, 1763, in Hanover County and saw the 27-year old Patrick Henry arguing for the Burgesses and against the King. The matter of law was settled; what was at stake was the extent of damages that the jury might award the particular contesting clergyman. That clergyman was of the opinion that the jury were of "the vulger herd," and his attorney agreed that amongst them were no "gentlemen." They were both right and in this the jury was surely a representative one.

Attorney Henry—certainly not discouraged by the presiding Judge, his father, John Henry—based his case on two points. One was the notoriously bad character which the colonial Anglican clergy had (something testified to by high dignitaries of that church); the other, and the weightier, was his insistence that in colonial affairs the colonial legislature was and should be supreme. Henry insisted that especially in the case of funds, raised in the colony and expended in the colony, the colonial assembly was sovereign and that the ruling of the Privy Council voiding such an act of the provincial assembly was unjust, and that an unjust ruling was itself, because it was unjust, null.

Of course, Henry well knew that the voiding of colonial acts had been done hundreds of times by the King in Council, but he knew, too, his Virginia and his fellow colonists and he knew that in expressing himself as he did—though the opposing attorney arose to shout, "the gentleman has spoken treason!"—he was expressing the sentiments of the overwhelming majority of his compatriots. Where "treasonous" views have such support, the ruler had best look to his power.

The jury, having no gentlemen, found for the complaining clergyman—and awarded him damages totalling one penny.

III

The writs of assistance case in Massachusetts shows still other aspects of colonial political strife. It arose due to an effort by the British government to enforce strictly its mercantilist regulations, as the Seven Years' War was drawing to a close and as the conquest of Canada reached completion. This coincided with the coming to the throne of George III, in October, 1760, and the appointment in August of the same year of a new—and it was hoped, by the British authorities, a more efficient—governor in Massachusetts, Francis Bernard.

The possibility of stricter enforcement of the imperial regulations presented itself with the closing years of the war, since now a large part of the Navy might be released from direct war services. Moreover, the war itself, by increasing the English debt, promising the elimination of the French threat and adding to the colonial possessions of Great Britain, all tended toward the attempted re-implementation, in new and strict forms, of the subordination and exploitation of the dangerously growing colonies.

Additionally, the British merchants and the British West Indian planters were bringing pressure to bear on the English government for such enforcement because the colonists were trading quite illegally with the French and Dutch West Indies—and had been doing so even while England was at war with France. Indeed, by the end of the 1750's, Rhode Island merchants were importing five times as much molasses from the foreign islands as from the British, while Massachusetts was importing almost 30 times as much from the foreign sources as from the British—and all of this was illegal trade! The molasses, in turn, was the raw product feeding the scores of rum distilleries in New England, and the manufacture of rum was by far the leading industrial enterprise in New England prior to the Revolution.[1]

The new Governor's efforts to enforce strictly the trade acts and customs regulations engendered strong resistance from the Boston merchants. As a result, his surveyor-general applied to the British Court of Exchequer for the issuance of writs of assistance —hitherto used in other parts of the realm—which were in effect general search warrants, empowering the official armed with them to search any home or ship for smuggled goods at any time and to compel bystanders to come to his assistance.

When the British court granted the request, the Governor turned to the colonial courts for its implementation and this seemed—in terms of law—to be nothing but a formal matter. The Boston merchants, however, deciding to resist the effort in the courts, combined their resources and at the close of 1760 hired two outstanding lawyers, Oxenbridge Thacher and James Otis, Jr., to argue their case. It was a clear sign of the times that Otis resigned his office as Advocate in the King's Vice-Admiralty court in favor of serving the merchants.

The case was heard by the Supreme Judicial Court in February, 1761. Thacher's argument was technical and, since the letter of the law clearly favored the Governor, not impressive. Otis— a son of the Speaker of the Colonial House of Representatives— chose an entirely different tack for his plea.

James Otis denied the validity of the Act of Parliament under which the writs were issued on two grounds: (1) that the act violated English common law or the Constitution; (2) that the act violated natural law. Therefore, reasoned Otis, it was the duty of the Court to deny the writs and to declare the relevant act a nullity.

The exact words of Otis were not transcribed, but his junior at the bar, John Adams, was present and made rough notes of what he heard. Before quoting from these, it is justice to Otis to state that Adams recorded that the advocate's words were delivered with "such a profusion of learning, such convincing argument, and such a torrent of sublime and pathetic eloquence, that a great crowd of spectators and auditors went away absolutely electrified."

"This writ," said Otis as recorded by Adams, "is against the fundamental principles of law. The privilege of the House. A man who is quiet, is as secure in his house, as a prince in his castle." A man's house, he went on, according to the English Constitution, was to be entered by officers of the law only "by a special warrant to search such a house, sworn to be suspected, and good grounds of suspicion appearing." With boldness, Otis continued:

> As to Acts of Parliament. An act against the Constitution is void; an act against natural equity is void; and if an act of Parliament should be made, in the very words of this petition, it would be void. The executive Courts must pass such acts into disuse.

Otis made the cause of the merchants, everyone's, for he held not only that writs of assistance were illegal in that they made search general, but also that, because they did, "it is a power that places the liberty of every man in the hands of every petty officer." It put a premium on vindictiveness; it exalted the informer; it was arbitrary, and "one arbitrary exertion [of power] will provoke another, until society be involved in tumult and in blood." Then Otis presented to the Court an actual instance, that had already occurred in Boston, even before the writs had been fully adjudicated, wherein the possessor of one of them had used its powers to wreak vengeance on a colonial judge and constable because they, in performing their duties, had done him harm.

Otis' arguments so impressed the Court as to lead to a delay of a year in the granting and exercising of the powers provided in the writs of assistance; so unpopular were they that in any case they were only sparingly employed. Moreover, on the basis of Otis' arguments other colonial courts, later, did refuse to grant the right to issue such writs.

Otis, himself, as a result of this effort, became the acknowledged leader of the now re-vitalized popular party—called the Country Party—and four months after his court appearance was elected to the Massachusetts House. There Otis, for a time, served as the foremost spokesman of the Country Party, which was an extension, into another generation, of the Land Bank Party led by Deacon Adams. Fitting it was, that Otis' right-hand man was Samuel Adams, son of the Deacon.

John Adams, years later, recorded in his diary that the effort of Otis against the writs of assistance was a turning point in his own life. "A contest appeared to me to be opened," he recalled, "to which I could foresee no end, and which would render my life a burden, and property, industry, and everything insecure." Then it was, wrote Adams, that he resolved,

> to take the side which appeared to be just, to march intrepidly forward in the right path, to trust in Providence for the protection of truth and right, and to die with a good conscience and a decent grace, if that trial should become indispensable.

Stirring words, indeed, from a man not easily stirred and not readily moved to emotional writing. Obviously, it was more than molasses that was involved, and more than making handsome fortunes from trading with whom and under whatever conditions one desired. Such trading was far from unimportant, of course, most particularly to 18th century New England merchants and to their workers dependent upon that trade for their livelihood.

But present here, too, were feelings of deep injustice and of colonial solidarity—of infringements upon a growing sense of oneness—of nationality, in fact, though the word was rarely used. Note, too, that Americans ruled by England found themselves increasingly impelled to appeal from the will of the King, and even from the will of Parliament—and after King and Parliament, surely nothing is left but nature and God (and the will of the people) and surely these are higher than either King or Parliament. They were high enough to stir John Adams.

Observe, too, that the advocate of the colonial merchants who were fighting to import molasses without restrictions, can, precisely because they were *colonial* merchants, invoke the cause of liberty in general. He could warn, quite correctly, that arbitrary infringements of their right to trade involved the infringements, as Otis said, of "the liberty of every man."

Chapter VII

Ideological Developments

THE COLONIES, BORN of capital-
ism, were born of Enlightenment, too. The technological development without which venturing forth to discover the New World
would have been impossible, and the socio-economic growth of
capitalism without which the impulse and the wherewithal to
conquer, to settle and to exploit that New World would have
been missing, themselves called forth and simultaneously came
out of—the process was dialectical—intellectual and scientific
advances. Seeing these advances in their material roots in no way
demeans them; it explains their origins, but does not detract
from their *significance*. These advances challenged the postulates
and assumptions of medieval intellectual life just as surely and
effectively as corresponding political and economic advances
challenged medieval life in those areas. And each advance fed,
in turn, the other.

I

The ideological revolution reflecting the material revolution that
sent Columbus across the seas in 1492, created the universality
of the genius of his contemporary, Leonardo da Vinci, who
insisted: "Nature is constrained by the reason of her law, which
lives infused in her." To master that law is to master her. And
this was the aim of the Enlightenment of the 16th and 17th
centuries—of the Spanish pioneer in psychology, Vives; of the

Polish builder of modern astronomy, Copernicus; of the Flemish trail-blazer in experimental anatomy, Vesalius; of the Italian founder of modern experimental science, Galileo; of the English exponent of experimentation and research, the inductive method of conquering truth, Francis Bacon; of the French conceiver of analytical geometry, Descartes.

The conviction that causality governed the world, and all its inhabitants, and the intention of mastering this causality was the well-spring of the Enlightenment. But the heart of it was humanist; the heart of it was the search for the laws of nature in order to serve mankind. From its origins, there is no neutrality in science in terms of whether or not it is to enhance the power and the freedom of humanity; this aim is modern science's ideological source. Summarizing his comments on the change from the medieval to the modern, the English scientist, J. D. Bernal, in his remarkable work, *Science in History,* writes: "Sublime contemplation had given way to profitable action."

The great objection raised by Francis Bacon against the medieval, authoritarian, deductive philosophy was that, "From all these systems . . . there can hardly after the lapse of so many years be adduced a single experiment which tends to *relieve and benefit the condition of man.*" But, he went on, "the true and lawful goal of the sciences is none other than this: that human life be endowed with new discoveries and powers." And, again "the improvement of man's lot and the improvement of man's mind are one and the same thing." The point, said Descartes, is that by mastering the laws of our universe, we may "render ourselves the masters and possessors of nature."

The new method and aim of the Enlightenment reflected its new view of man and his society. The Enlightenment challenged the static, hierarchical essence of medievalism—"I can listen only with the greatest repugnance," said Galileo, "when the quality of unchangeability is held up as something preeminent and complete in contrast to variability." It challenged the former virtues of subordination and submissiveness; of bearing meekly the terrible burdens of this life as a testing of one's faith and thus a testing of one's worthiness to be saved.[1] It denied that Man is a damned worm, impotent, sinful and worthless. On the contrary, wrote Shakespeare:

> What a piece of work is man! how noble to reason! how infinite in faculties! in form and moving how express and admirable! in action how like an angel! in apprehension how like a god!

Above all, perhaps, it represented the rejection of dogma, the refusal to accept on faith; the insistence that everything—no matter what its authority—required reasonable examination. "To reach the truth one must," asserted Descartes, "once in one's life, dispense with all received opinions, and reconstruct anew and from the foundations all one's system of knowledge."

It produced efforts to rationalize international relations and to limit warfare, as enunciated by the Dutch jurist, Hugo Grotius (Huigh de Groot, a political prisoner condemned to a life term, who escaped confinement and lived out his days in exile, dying in France in 1645) and developed further by the German, von Pufendorf and the Swiss philosophers, Burlamaqui and De Vattel. Each of these men, too, appealed to a natural law held to be superior to the will of any particular sovereign, and justified revolution where the acts of the sovereign contravened natural law. All of them, but especially Burlamaqui, stressed, also, that through man's reason he might achieve happiness, and all affirmed that it was this achievement which was the central purpose of human existence.

They were all known to and influential among the leaders of American colonial society. Quite naturally, however, it was the writers in English who were most avidly read by them; these included, in addition to Bacon, such figures as Thomas More, James Harrington, Thomas Hobbes, Richard Hooker, John Milton, Algernon Sidney, and—above all—Isaac Newton and John Locke. These men differed, of course, in many respects, but in their kinship to the Enlightenment they were one—in their dependence upon reasoned argument, upon scientific investigation, they were one; in their assumption of the reality of

causation they were one; in their concern with the mundane
welfare of mankind they were one; in their view of the State as
man-derived and as intended to service man they were one; and
in their view of the possibility of progress they were one. It may
be added, as also relevant to the colonists, that many of them
were political heretics, suffering jail, exile and—in the cases of
More and Sidney—execution.

II

In the American colonies the ideas of the Enlightenment spread
rapidly. Here was a land whose birth was a product of the
movement from feudalism to capitalism; hence it was to be
expected that the philosophical offspring of that revolution
would find welcome here. Here, too, was a society made up of a
composite of many nations and many religions so that toleration
of dissent and of variety became a necessity of existence. This
helped develop the idea not merely of toleration but of freedom
of opinion as most salutary to all concerned.

Here, too, was a land of near illimitable size and resources
whose population doubled and tripled every decade and whose
very growth made swift change a commonplace and seemed
to bring reality to the philosophical musings concerning progress.
And this land with its preoccupation in conquering its wildness
and resources and developing its economy and its cities encouraged technical and scientific inquiry and development,
which in turn fought against orthodoxy and inculcated the need
to wrest from nature its mysteries.

Furthermore, the very newness of the land gave it from the
earliest days something of the reputation of a haven for the
exploited and a harbor for the persecuted. (It was characteristic
that More's Utopia was in America.) This induced the immigration to the New World of pietistic and radical sects, springing
up throughout Europe as the bourgeois national revolutions
swept on—migrations which in turn furthered the development
of equalitarian and libertarian ideas in the colonies.

Moreover, all this was true of a colonial land whose development enhanced the antagonisms with the imperial power; and many of the propertied here were naturally attracted to libertarian and equalitarian ideas as justifications for their own aspirations. These ideas, so encouraged, found ready enough welcome among the non-propertied masses. These masses in insisting that the ideas applied to themselves—and in so applying, often extended them—frequently terrified the very merchants and planters who had announced themselves as "Enlightened."

The vested authorities charged with maintaining the colonial relationship sought to restrain the colonists intellectually as well as economically and politically; and many among the colonial rich, though indeed colonials, were torn by fear of the masses and by devotion to the respectability and "order" that came from the Empire. They also frequently played a restraining role when it came to letting the fresh breezes ruffle the stuffiness of the past. Struggle, then, was characteristic of the intellectual history of the colonial era as it was of every other aspect.

Much of the best of the colonial development is summed up in the ideas of the "brace of Adamses" in their youth—a youth forged by the whole preceding century of turmoil and one heralding the overthrow of the colonial status (something very largely accomplished—as is characteristic of colonial revolutions —by the youth). Samuel Adams submitted, as his graduation thesis in Harvard, in 1743, when he was 21 years old, an examination of "The Doctrine of the Lawfulness of Resistance to the Supreme Magistrate if the Commonwealth Cannot Otherwise be Preserved." Needless to say, his examination led him to conclude that the "doctrine" was quite sound.

John Adams, graduating Harvard at the age of 20, began his career as a grammar school teacher in Worcester. While there, in 1755, he wrote to a friend: "All that part of creation which lies within our observation, is liable to change. Even mighty states and kingdoms are not exempted." Young John Adams went on to make clear that he had in mind specifically the "mighty state" of England, for he thought that "the great seat of empire" was going to be transferred "into America." Only one thing, he wrote, could "keep us from setting up for ourselves" and that was "to disunite us . . . to keep us in distinct colonies." Six months later the young man was confiding to his diary even more stirring thoughts of the prowess of Man, and of how it opened up limitless vistas of advance through the mastery of nature:

> Man . . . by the exercise of his reason can invent engines and instruments, to take advantage of the powers in nature, and accomplish the most astonishing designs. He can rear the valley into a lofty mountain, and reduce the mountain to a humble vale. He can rend the rocks and level the proudest trees.

Yes, said the young John Adams, man is able to and will unravel the mysteries of the minutest entities "that escape the observation of our naked sight" and even "of the regions of heaven" itself.

Thus was the spirit of the Enlightenment—epitomized in the realization that all is subject to change and that nature's laws can be mastered by man for his greater happiness—combined with a rudimentary sense of nationalism, forging the revolutionary patriot.

III

But this advanced position had to be arrived at in face of the established authorities who held the opposite and who had the power to make disagreement with them more than an academic matter. The favorite texts of these authorities were provided by their most influential spiritual forces—the Anglican clergy—to wit: *Proverbs* 24:21: "My son, fear thou the Lord and the king; and meddle not with them that are given to change"; and, even more frequently cited, *Romans* 13: 1-2: ". . . the powers that be are ordained of God. Whosoever therefore resisteth the power, resisteth the ordinance of God: and they that resist shall receive to themselves damnation."

But the dissenting clergy—and they dominated the religious scene in most of the American colonies—were sufficiently children of the Enlightenment to teach that God himself was bound by the laws of Nature and of Right, which were indeed His Laws and thus had to be agreeable to him. God himself could not, for he would not, violate these laws, and had covenanted that he would not; hence, when any of his temporal agents—be they kings or tide-waiters—violated these laws of nature and of righteousness, when they became oppressive, they were in fact tyrannical and acting outside the law. Obedience in such cases was slavery, not loyalty. Obedience in such cases was acquiescence in the violation of God's will and of nature's law; it was sinful and shameful; hence resistance to tyrants was quite literally obedience to God.[2]

The expression of God's will in man's dealing one with the other came in government, and this government expressed the collective desires and needs of God's images, of man. Hence government was an agreement, a compact, to advance the glory of God and the well-being of Man. Hence, too, the voice of the People is the will of God, and a ruler defied either at mortal and immortal peril. Thus, by 1733, a Harvard Commencement thesis is entitled: "Is the Voice of the People the Voice of God?" and is resolved affirmatively.

Yet several cautionary remarks are necessary. First, the People, to the dominant philosophers and political thinkers of the 16th and 17th (and for the most part, 18th century too) was composed of all *except* the masses—who might be referred to as "inhabitants" or the "vulgar" or the "poor," but not as the People. "People" were propertied, were those with a "stake" in society and hence those who should have some voice in its administration. Equality did not encompass even the formal political equality of the toilers. For, said a sermon preached by Edward Holyoke in Massachusetts in 1736—and typical of prevailing views: "There are men who because of their occupations, cannot get knowledge which fits them for public position." That these included the bulk of the (male) population is clear when the minister spelled out that he had in mind those who "holdeth the Plough and glorieth in the goad, that driveth oxen and are occupied in their labors, and whose talk is of bullocks."

This was related to the anti-democratic assumption, rarely questioned in published material, that in each society a few were the rulers and the majority were the ruled. Thus, in reading a typical expression of the right to resist oppressive sovereignty—for instance, Joseph Moss' sermon of 1715, holding "the people must submit to the rulers, so long as rulers keep within legal limits"—there should not be so much attention upon the qualifying clause as to overlook that which is qualified— namely the propriety of the "people's" submission to their rulers. John Cotton thought it sufficient to refute democracy by asking: "If the people be governors, who shall be governed?" Levelism was the ultimate heresy.

There was nothing subtle in the oligarchy's expression of its class consciousness. Typical is the work of John Winthrop— leader of the Massachusetts Bay colony during its first 20 years —entitled *A Model of Christian Charity* (1630). Here is developed the prevalent idea that every society necessarily divides itself into two classes—the rich and the poor—and that, of course, the first are the able and the rulers, while the second are the incompetent and the ruled.

Reinforcing the bias of most of the dissenting churches was their insistence, so significant a part of their break from the feudal Catholic hegemony, that riches was godliness; that, indeed, a key demonstration of being among the Elect was worldly success vouchsafed by the Lord, and the more of it, the more certain the Election! Thus, poverty was, quite literally, damning, and the Elect resembled very much the modern Elite.

Thus, here are the words of John Winthrop, in the aforementioned sermon:

> God Almighty in His most holy and wise providence hath so disposed of the condition of mankind as in all times some must be rich, some poor; some high and eminent in power and dignity, others mean and in subjection.

In explaining the reasons for this allegedly immutable and divine condition, John Winthrop said, among other things:

> That He might have the more occasion to manifest the work of His Spirit: first, upon the wicked in moderating and restraining them, so that the rich and mighty should not eat up the poor, nor the poor and despised rise up against their superiors and shake off their yoke; secondly, in the regenerate, in exercising His graces in them—as in the great ones, their love, mercy, gentleness, temperance, etc., in the poor and inferior sort, their faith, patience, obedience, etc.

Finally, when the dissenting churches became potent—or established, as in Massachusetts and Connecticut—they became themselves ramparts of conservatism and exponents of fierce intolerance. Of course, while most of the intellectual ferment took on a religious covering—since the age was ecclesiastical and since the church establishments were so central a part of the cultural and political life of the times—much of this ferment nevertheless appeared in outright political garb.

To offer a closer and more specific examination of this phase of colonial life and history, we shall select several salient phenomena and try to explain them in their times and places. To this end, we shall examine certain highly revealing episodes of struggle against the New England theological oligarchy including those involving Roger Williams, Anne Hutchinson, the Salem witch-hunt, John Wise and the "Great Awakening." And we shall also examine certain political controversies, notably that involving the editor, John Peter Zenger, for the light these shed on the state of intellectual development in the colonial period.

Chapter VIII

Williams, Hutchinson and the Witch - Hunt

I

V ERNON L. PARRINGTON, in his classical study of *The Colonial Mind,* pioneered in bringing forward the giant figure of Roger Williams. Yet, in performing this sterling service, Parrington tended to isolate Williams from the mainstream of his time and so to distort both the man and the era. Williams, wrote Parrington: "lived and dreamed in a future he was not to see, impatient to bring to men a heaven they were unready for. And because they were unready they could not understand the grounds of his hope, and not understanding they were puzzled and angry and cast him out to dream his dreams in the wilderness."

But not "man" in general cast Williams out—it was the ruling class of the Massachusetts colony that banished him. And Williams, having been banished, did not dream out his dreams in the wilderness; on the contrary, several from Massachusetts who likewise opposed that class, went with him in the first weeks and many more soon thereafter followed him—not only from Massachusetts, but also from England—and together they made of the wilderness, the colony of Rhode Island. Parrington's sentences convey the idea of Williams as the noble, but impractical thinker; but the fact is, as Clinton Rossiter has pointed out, "an unusually close connection between theory and practice marked both his mind and career."

The decisive significance of Roger Williams does not lie in his uniqueness, nor in the banishment visited upon him for his advanced ideas. It lies, rather, in the organic tie between those advanced ideas and his time and place which is demonstrated by practical successes he achieved—with the help of many people—in putting into effect his ideas. In this sense Williams' career is especially illuminating of American colonial history.

In considering the equalitarianism of Williams and his opposition to a church-state tie and his call for freedom of conscience, it is relevant to recall that all this is present in Sir Thomas More's *Utopia* (1516)—set, let it be remembered, in America. "One of the ancientest laws," in Utopia, wrote More, provided

> that no man shall be blamed for reasoning in the maintenance of his religion . . . nor they constrain him not with threatenings to dissemble his mind, and show countenance contrary to his thought. For deceit and falsehood and all manner of lies, as next unto fraud, they do marvelously reject and abhor.

Moreover, in this Utopia, the rich do not rob the poor, and all live in common and help each other (even as did the Indians, Roger Williams was to write admiringly) all of which was passing wonderful, wrote More, for

> when I consider and weigh in my mind all these Commonwealths which nowadays anywhere do flourish so, God help me, I can perceive nothing but a certain conspiracy of rich men procuring their own commodities, under the name and title of the Commonwealth.

It should be pointed out—and Max Savelle has done this in his admirable study of colonial intellectual and cultural life, *Seeds of Liberty*—that many of Williams' English contemporaries and friends were developing concepts of religious toleration and of the propriety of separating church from state. This was, of course, part of the whole historic break against feudalism.

Of great importance in explaining the growing favor with which the rulers of Great Britain viewed religious toleration, is the fact that such toleration served to attract settlers in the colonial areas—which the Proprietors in particular welcomed—and because its absence tended to hurt the free development of trade—which the merchants especially wanted. Thus, the Proprietors, in their propaganda seeking to attract settlers from Europe always stressed three things: a liberal land policy; a mild government, religious liberty. As for the trading aspect, note these words in a communication from the Lords of Trade in London to the President of the Council in Virginia, written September 1, 1750: "As Toleration and a free exercise of religion is so valuable a branch of true liberty, and so essential to the enriching and improving of a Trading Nation; it should ever be held sacred in his Majesties Colonies."

Oliver Cromwell himself was wondering aloud: "Is it ingenuous to ask for [religious] liberty and not to give it?" John Milton was developing his ideas of religious toleration—confined, it is true, to Protestants—and, in 1641, announced his refusal to take the "loyalty oath" newly required by the harassed Charles I, in these words:

> Perceiving what tyranny had invaded the Church—that he who would take orders must subscribe slave, and take an oath withal, which unless he took with a conscience that would retch, he must either perjure or split his faith—I thought it better to prefer a blameless silence before the sacred office of speaking, bouth and begun with servitude and forswearing.

Sir Henry Vane, a parliamentary leader in the struggle against Charles, who had himself been in Massachusetts and was well acquainted with Williams, was writing, as to church and state, exactly what Williams believed: "The magistrate had no right to go beyond matters of outward practice, converse, and dealings in the things of this life between man and man."

Moreover, much of the European continent was witnessing the appearance of similar questioning. It was the period of the Collegiants, the Generalists, the Familists, the Antinomians, the

Friends, the Seekers—of Hans Denck, Valentine Weigel, Jacob Boehme, Giles Randall, George Fox—and Roger Williams.

All deprecated dogma, authoritarianism, and ceremony. All emphasized the Light, the Spirit, or the Word as the most important source of contact with God. All believed in the possibility of conquering sin. Many drew definite social implications from these ideas, such as the denunciation of religious persecution, or the condemnation of the economic and political subordination of the mass of the people. Most advanced among these were the so-called Levellers—men like John Lilburne, William Walwyn, and Richard Overton—whose writings were appearing simultaneously with those of Roger Williams and were conveying, in considerable part, similar arguments and programs.

In the Massachusetts of the 1630's, when Roger Williams was there, social unrest and intellectual ferment were characteristic in the face of the ecclesiastical oligarchy of Winthrop and Cotton. It was in 1630, one year prior to Williams' arrival, that the dissenting merchant and trader, Thomas Morton, was banished to England by that oligarchy for subversive conduct and dangerous thoughts. Not unusual was the punishment of one Phillip Ratcliffe, in 1631, sentenced to "be whipped, have his ears cut off, fined 40 shillings, and banished," for the crime of "uttering malicious and scandalous speeches against the government and the Church."

Williams lived in Massachusetts at a time when the political struggle of the freemen of the colony against the iron grip of the handful of rulers was at a highpoint. It was in 1633 that the minority which was enfranchised voted that the Governor and his aides were to be elected annually, and that each town was to appoint two delegates to function with them in the levying of taxes.

The next year these freemen went further, and demanded that Governor Winthrop and the General Court abide by the rules of the original charter which gave to the whole body of freemen the right to participate in the making of laws. Governor Winthrop and the clergy led by John Cotton—who controlled the suffrage since they held the power of admission to the church and only members could vote—fought desperately against this demand, but without success. Representative government—of a very limited kind, with yet a minute elite in power, it is true—thus came to Massachusetts, and the General Court, consisting of the Governor, his assistants and the town-elected deputies, was to have the right to admit freemen, lay taxes, and pass laws.

The oligarchy emerged still dominant, but not unchallenged, not without having yielded some, and not without having been badly frightened. Indeed, the 1634 election in Boston had a distinct class struggle flavor to it, with the inhabitants fearful that "the richer men would give the poorer sort no great proportions of land"—a pertinent fear indeed, since Governor Winthrop had generously staked himself to 1,800 acres, and his class brothers were not far behind—Dudley with 1,700 and Saltonstall with 1,600 acres. It is as a part of all this that the dire challenges of Roger Williams, and others, appeared.

Notwithstanding the fact that so eminent an authority as Perry Miller in his study of *The New England Mind* insists that the 17th century struggle in Massachusetts was "fought not by persons who objected on principle to the dictatorial or undemocratic rule of the saints, but by adherents of religious views at variance with the established orthodoxy," we find such a view excessively narrow. Miller, in his more recent biography of Roger Williams, applies this same constricting view to that personage in particular, and finds that Williams "actually exerted little or no influence on institutional developments in America"; that advances in religious liberties later achieved were gained on "wholly other grounds" than those advanced by Williams, and that celebrating him "as the prophet of religious freedom" provides him with an "ill-fitting halo." [1]

Miller was anxious to correct anachronistic renderings of Roger Williams and his time, which offered both in 20th century terms. Certainly this is erroneous and mechanical, but in correcting, Miller has gone much too far and has made history discontinuous. He has emphasized the unique at the expense of the common and the related.

The fact is that Williams' own contemporaries saw his attacks, as Cotton Mather said, as aimed at "the whole political, as well as ecclesiastical constitution of the country." The fact is that John Winthrop, in his *Journal in* 1645, stated that, "The great questions that have troubled the country are about the authority of the magistrates and the liberty of the people."

Of course, Winthrop was speaking of religious liberty, but church and state were one in his world and mind, and the magistrates were the ministers' instruments. So that Williams' attacks did go to the root of the political and economic and ideological structure of the society of his time and it did have profound and lasting effects on that society and time. Those effects were of the greatest moment in the "institutional developments" not only, and decisively, in terms of Rhode Island, but also in terms of all New England, and eventually of the United States as a whole.

At the same time, in saying this, one must not ignore the decisive power and influence of the Winthrops and the Mathers and the Cottons, on their own time and upon the future. Perry Miller is largely correct, I think, when he says that one like the Reverend John Cotton was "the incarnation of that image of respectability, conformity, success . . . which has since dominated American spiritual and intellectual life." I would qualify the domination and add the element of struggle against "respectability" which has been so large a component of the American tradition—and of which Roger Williams is so magnificent an example. Yet, it is true that in concentrating on Williams and his trials and his vindication, there develops a tendency to underplay the reality of the lasting influence of the Cottons—which actually means misinterpreting the Williamses too.

Williams really believed that "God had made of one blood" all mankind, and to him all people were equal in the sight of God and hence should find equal treatment at the hands of His children. In this he included *all* people of all colors and persuasions. Especially notable was the fact that he included the American Indians (Williams wrote the first Indian-English dictionary), and that he drew the necessary but very provocative conclusion that the forcible taking of their lands was sinful and therefore void, thus questioning the King's title and all other land titles—questioning, indeed, the whole base of the Massachusetts economy.

He demanded the complete separation of church and state, and attacked with great forcefulness "the bloody doctrine of persecution for the cause of conscience," thus assaulting the ideological base of the theocratic oligarchy in Massachusetts.[2] He was far from indifferent, of course, in matters of religion; but he insisted that *all*, even "the most paganish, Jewish, Turkish, or antichristian consciences and worships," be freely permitted and not be the cause of any persecution whatever.

He specifically rejected the right of the oligarchy to impose a loyalty oath upon all residents of the colony and said that he himself would not subscribe to it. He held such oaths to be blasphemous and urged the members of his Salem church to oppose it.

Roger Williams taught that "the sovereign, original and foundation of civil power lies in the people," wherefrom it followed that:

> a people may erect and establish what form of Government seems to them most meet for their civil condition. It is evident that such Governments as are by them erected and established, have no more power, nor for any longer time, than the civil power or people consenting and agreeing shall betrust them with.

Nor did he vitiate this view by holding, as did the Cottons, that while all power derived from the people, this applied essentially only to regenerate people, who naturally (especially if they were regenerate) would want to do God's will. Wanting this, they would know that it was the Magistrates who were God's instruments for implementing that will, wherefore the people's will would be God's will as known to and stated by his servants—*i.e.,* the oligarchy!

The state, he held, must touch only behavior, not conscience; and its concern must be with the welfare and the peace of its inhabitants. Such a state was necessary (Williams rejected anarchy); and only such a state was in accord with God's will.

Williams, after hearings and trial, was sentenced to banishment, for he "hath broached and divulged diverse new and dangerous opinions, against the authority of magistrates." At first the execution of banishment was postponed to let the winter pass, but on condition that Williams refrain from meeting with the people of Salem. The people, however, sought him out for they loved him and favored him, wherefore officers were sent to arrest him at once. In Cotton's words: "His corrupt imagination provoked the magistrates rather than to breed a winter's spiritual plague in the country to put upon him a winter's journey out of the country."

It had only been with severe pressures upon his Salem congregation (including the threat to withhold needed land from the town) that the magistrates had succeeded in getting Williams' church to discharge him. Even so, a large minority remained his partisans, and within the first months after he was banished and made his way to present Rhode Island (he named the place where he settled, Providence) 60 persons followed him, and within a few years several thousands had come to the new Canaan. Special mention must be made of Mrs. Williams, who, raising six children and enduring with Williams his life of suffering and privation, remained throughout his staunch ally and support.

II

After many tribulations, Williams succeeded in getting a charter for his Rhode Island, and in parrying several threats of invasion from Massachusetts, whose rulers wanted to forcibly wipe out "Rogues Island." In 1647 an instrument of government was set up for Williams' colony which made of it by far the most democratic form of government then in existence. In it slavery and indentured servitude were forbidden (though the former prohibition did not remain effective in the 18th century). The entire penal code was made very much more humane than that existing in England or any of its other colonies. Imprisonment for debt was abolished, provided only that the debtor agreed to a course of payment. Land was purchased honestly from the Indians and a model of fair dealing was established with the result of unbroken friendship and peace. The engrossing of land was forbidden, and complete freedom of religion and conscience for all was established. Rhode Island was declared a place of refuge for all suffering for conscience's sake, and there, indeed, Jews and Quakers and even "witches" did find a haven and equality and fraternity. The compact setting up this government—and it was done by an assemblage of the majority of the male inhabitants—was explicitly declared to be "democratical, that is to say, a Government held by the free and voluntary consent of all, or the greater part of the free inhabitants."

All officers were elected yearly and subject to recall. The English code of law was adopted, but there was specific denial of favored treatment on the grounds of "good" birth.

While Williams' views of complete equality did not include the political liberation of women, as was true of the Quakers also, it did encompass an insistence upon their equality in the eyes of God, and their full rights to have opinions of their own and to express and support them. Notable in this connection was the case of Goodman Viner who, in 1638, attempted to prevent his wife from attending religious meetings that displeased him. Mrs. Viner, however, insisted on her right to believe as she pleased and when her husband used violence to impose his will, Rhode Island disfranchised him and impelled him to leave—thus revoking the husband's "freedom" to keep his wife in subjection, despite certain good biblical authority for such behavior.

Of course, private ownership was not disturbed but rather encouraged and protected, and with this, as the decades wore on, engrossment of, and speculation in, land did occur. Thus, there developed more and more economic inequality and a consequent growth of political inequality,[3] until indeed, in the 19th century, Rhode Island's political apparatus was quite retarded, even from the point of view of bourgeois democracy.

The fact remains, nonetheless, that Roger Williams was one of the most advanced, consistent, and successful friends of freedom that American history has yet produced; one who, in his time, had few peers and no superiors in devotion to the well-being of humanity.

III

In the same years that Roger Williams was contesting the power of the Massachusetts oligarchy, other men and women were doing the same, and also splitting away from its domination. Most notable were the Reverend Thomas Hooker, Mrs. Anne Hutchinson, Mrs. Catherine Scott and Ezekiel Holloman—(the latter two founders of the first Baptist church in 1637)—John Wheelwright, William Coddington, John Clarke, and Samuel Gorton.

Hooker, who had come to Massachusetts in 1633, was a minister in Newton (the present Cambridge) and a leading figure in the Massachusetts oligarchy. He it was, in fact, who was entrusted with the onerous task of debating and confuting Williams' heresies. Nevertheless, he, and most of his flock, felt it necessary to leave by 1636 because they finally found the absolutism of the Mathers and Cottons too much.

While it is quite wrong to equate the position of Hooker with that of Williams, in terms of a democratic and equalitarian orientation—as Parrington did, and, more recently, Carleton Beals does—it is nevertheless also erroneous to take the position of Perry Miller that Hooker represented no break at all with the oligarchy. He did favor a more representative government and he did disagree with Winthrop, who held that of the body of the people "the best part is always the least, and of that part the wiser part is always the lesser." On the contrary, replied Hooker: "A general counsel chosen by all, I conceive under favor most suitable to rule and most safe for the relief of the people." The Fundamental Orders (adopted January, 1639) under which was set up Hooker's Connecticut, while to the Right politically and ideologically of Williams' system, nevertheless was more representative of a wider body of people and more responsive to their desires than was the Massachusetts system.

The ideas of the remarkable Mrs. Hutchinson and her numerous followers represented one of the most serious threats to domination that the theocracy ever faced. Mrs. Hutchinson, a close friend of the Reverend John Cotton, settled in Boston in 1634. She early began the habit of holding collective discussions of central philosophical and religious problems. As a result she came to the conclusion that the Bible taught salvation through a covenant of grace and not a covenant of works. Mrs. Hutchinson, not unlike the Quakers who were also to shake the foundations of the theocracy and move it to depths of sadism, was maintaining that an inner light was the basic truth of the religious experience. She was saying that the religious experience was individual and personal, and did not require formalized study, let alone ministerial guidance or domination.

Or, as a follower of Mrs. Hutchinson put it: "I had rather hear such a one speak that speaks from a mere motion of the spirit, without any study at all, than any of your learned scholars, although they may be full of scripture." Notice that "such a one" might include a woman, and that in this case the leader of the heresy was a woman. Indeed, not the least of the charges against Mrs. Hutchinson was that her sedition was compounded, for not only did her ideas tend to subvert the oligarchy, but *she* insisted on making vocal these ideas and thus, as a mere woman, was presuming equality with men and indeed was insisting that she had something to teach men.

Something of the force of this consideration may be gathered from a contemporaneous remark of Governor John Winthrop. In his journal under date April 13, 1645, the Governor wrote:

Mr. Hopkins, the governor of Hartford upon Connecticut, came to Boston, and brought his wife with him (a godly young woman, and of special parts), who was fallen into a sad infirmity, the loss of her understanding and reason, which had been growing upon her divers years, by occasion of her giving herself wholly to reading and writing, and had written many books. Her husband, being very loving and tender of her, was loath to grieve her; but he saw his error, when it was too late. For if she had attended her household duties, and such things as belong to women, and not gone out of her way and calling to meddle in such things as are proper for men, whose minds are stronger, etc., she had kept her wits, and might have improved them usefully and honorably in the place God had set her.

And about the same time, Mrs. Anne Bradstreet, the leading 17th century New England poet—wife of one governor and daughter of another—had written:

> *I am obnoxious to each carping tongue*
> *Who says my hand a needle better fits,*
> *A poet's pen all scorn I should thus wrong,*
> *For such despite they cast on female wits:*
> *If what I do prove well, it won't advance,*
> *They'll say it's stolen, or else it was by chance.*

That the challenge came from a woman, then, was a decisive element, though underrated in the literature on the subject, explaining the hierarchy's assessment of Mrs. Hutchinson as an especially dangerous "subversive." But, of course, her ideas and not her sex were decisive. And those ideas represented, in the words of Perry Miller, a kind of "spiritual anarchy"; where church and state were united such anarchy approached uncomfortably close to a political one, too.[4]

The Hutchinson view had great popular support, particularly in Boston, and it took many months of careful maneuvering by the oligarchy before it could bring in a verdict of heresy, which meant sedition and carried with it the sentence of banishment. Some of these political exiles joined Williams to help found Rhode Island, some went elsewhere, a few even as far north as present Maine and New Hampshire. Others, returning to Massachusetts, were executed.

Within the context of early 17th century England, and the movements in the New World symbolized by the names Roger Williams and Anne Hutchinson, one may better understand the promulgation, in 1641, in Massachusetts Bay, of the Body of Liberties. Governor Winthrop noted in 1639 that the inhabitants "had long desired a body of laws, and thought their condition very unsafe while so much power rested in the discretion of the magistrates." This "desire" and the critical pressures manifested by a Williams and a Hutchinson, induced the rulers of the colony to issue this Body of Liberties.

While in this code certain of the Liberties were in fact restricted to Protestants adhering to the Congregational form of worship, it did provide unto "every person within this jurisdiction, whether inhabitant or foreigner" certain individual rights and protections. Thus, the governing powers were forbidden to deprive anyone of life, liberty or property without due process of law; and all were specifically declared to be entitled to the equal protection of the law.

Habeas corpus proceedings were provided and "inhumane, barbarous or cruel" punishments were outlawed (though what *was* then permitted indicates a change in definitions of "cruelty"). To convict of a capital crime, the testimony of two witnesses was necessary. All freemen were guaranteed the right of petition, and the free exercise of religion, within the severe limits stated above. Monopolies were outlawed and forced military service outside the bounds of the colony was prohibited.

Annual elections for every township were provided, and the common-law privilege granted husbands of physically "correcting" their wives was forbidden. A husband was forbidden to offer any violence to his wife, "unless it be in his own defence under her assault." Emigration outside the borders of the colony was recognized as the right of any of its inhabitants.

This advanced body of law influenced the passage of similar enactments by other colonies, as Connecticut. It was of consequence, too, as Robert A. Rutland has shown, as one of the home-grown precedents culminating in the American Bill of Rights.

IV

Angels of darkness and angels of light were as real to the European civilization of the 16th and 17th centuries as was God Himself. No less a personage than Martin Luther had told in detail of his encounter with an emissary of the devil, and had explained that he had driven the evil one off by flinging an inkwell at him.

Mystery was everywhere and the supernatural served as explanation. Hardship, pain and suffering were everywhere, too, and if solutions were sought in mundane arrangements, the searchings could be most unpleasant for those ruling such arrangements. Hence, angels of darkness made their appearance at moments of general distress and catastrophe; they were indeed the agencies of such distress and catastrophes. To exorcise them was to be a social engineer as well as an effective heavenly agent. That challenges to the status quo were literally devilish made their refutation simpler; it did not necessarily mean that the refuters were demagogic.

The "Fundamentals" or "Body of Liberties" ratified in 1641 for the Massachusetts Bay colony established twelve capital crimes and among them was witchcraft—in accordance with the biblical injunction: "Suffer ye not witches to live." In this provision the colony was in accord with the law of all Europe, and, indeed, of all Christendom.

This law was implemented as part of the Puritan oligarchy's effort to maintain its position; and when the position was seriously threatened, the law was re-discovered afresh. This happened, for example, in the 1650's in the face of the threats arising from Rhode Island blasphemy and sedition and from Quaker radicalism. It happened with a vengeance in the late 1680's and early 1690's, and that is a story worth some recounting.

The witchhunting terror of these years was instituted by a desperate ruling class which found its grip on power more and more seriously threatened. It did not "originate in the childish fantasies of some very little girls" as its latest chronicler, Marion L. Starkey, maintains in the course of her efforts "to review the records in the light of the findings of modern psychology, particularly of the Freudian school." So long as there are children, there will be "childish fantasies" but of what they consist and what interest they arouse and how they are interpreted and to what uses they may be put will not depend upon little girls.

Nor will it do to label the Ministers, as did Parrington, the "blind leaders of the blind [who] lent their sanction to the intolerance of the mass judgment," thus, in fact, putting the onus on the masses; this is done another way by Miss Starkey who credits the overcoming of the terror to "the stubborn refusal of the few to give way to the hysteria and mad logic of the many."

It was not the "many" who presided at the witch-hunting trials; it was Lieutenant-Governor Stoughton. It was the élite who established and constituted the witch-hunting committee that toured Massachusetts villages looking for witches and condemning them. It was the President of Harvard who wrote learned proofs of the reality of witchery and the necessity to extirpate it; it was his Minister son who followed with other learned proofs, and these were countersigned by the leading dignitaries of the colony.

It was the state apparatus and propaganda apparatus of the rulers which called into being the witch-hunting hysteria and sought to sustain that hysteria; and it was their officials who jailed and tortured and executed the witches. It was the élite who remained dissatisfied with mere "confessions" and insisted that the confessions to be real must be followed by the names of fellow agents of the devil—and that only then would the confessor be spared execution. It was the élite, too, who expressed horror when some of the confessors—unable to live with their lie and appalled at the suffering their "confessions" caused—retracted; in such cases it was the élite who refused to believe the

retractions, found them evidences of devilish allegiance and proceeded to execute the conscience-stricken informers. Indeed, the
evidence shows that in this case—as in the case of the persecution of the Quakers a generation earlier—*it was popular disgust
and protest that helped call a halt to the bloody proceedings.*

Professor Wertenbaker has pointed convincingly to the connection between the institution by the theocracy of this reign of
terror and its own realization that power was slipping from its
grasp. By 1650 ministers were distressed at the growing influence
of the merchants who, as one divine then remarked, would "tol-
erate diverse kinds of sinful opinions to entice men to come and
sit down with us, that their purses might be filled with coin"
though at the same time the government might be filled "with
contention, and the Church of our Lord Christ with errors."
Some years later, the Reverend John Higginson, in an Election
Sermon, felt obliged to warn: "New England is originally a
plantation of religion, not a plantation of trade and such as are
increasing cent per cent remember this."

Cotton Mather, in his very influential history of New England, *Magnalia Christi Americana,*[5] recounts that in the same
period a minister was preaching in northeastern Massachusetts
and that he was urging his auditors to continue "a religious
people from this consideration that otherwise they would con-
tradict the main end of planting this wilderness," whereupon he
was interrupted—an unheard of affront in itself—by "a well-
known person" in the congregation who "cried out, Sir, you are
mistaken—our main end was to catch fish."

Everything then—from Roger Williams and his accursed, but
flourishing Rhode Island, to this impudent fisherman—pointed
to an increased secularization in Massachusetts life and an increased challenge to the repressive hold of the theocracy. The
process was furthered with the development of English politics
leading James II to consolidate all the New England colonies
(and later New York and the Jerseys) into the Dominion of
New England (1686). This resulted in the appointment of a
very unpopular Royal Governor, Sir Edmund Andros, and the

voiding of colonial charters and governmental institutions, including those dominated by the Massachusetts theocracy.

With the overthrow of Andros, in 1689 (a counterpart of the overthrow of James II), the ministers attempted to reinstitute the oligarchic control they had had, prior to Andros, but they were only partially successful. Thus, in 1691 a new charter was granted Massachusetts, but under it the colony became a royal government, not unlike that of Virginia, with a representative assembly, and with the franchise based not on church membership but on property ownership. Simultaneously, religious freedom for all Protestants was guaranteed.

Clearly, for Cotton Mather and his brethren, as he wrote in his *Wonders of the Invisible World* (1693), "An army of Devils is horribly broke in upon the place." He and those like him were intent on discovering tangible evidences of the work of these devils that would convince even the most skeptical and would return all doubters to the true faith—under the aegis of the keepers of the faith, *i.e.*, the Reverend Mathers, *et al.* The more terrible and the more widespread the evidence, the better.

V

It is at this moment, in 1688, that the strange behavior of four children in Boston attracted the scrutiny of Cotton Mather himself. The children gave every evidence of being possessed and under sharp and continued questioning finally accused an aged indentured servant (who, incidentally, had scolded one of the children for having accused her own child of theft) of being a witch. The woman was tried, convicted and hanged.

But that would not end it for the learned son of the most prominent minister of Boston. Rather he decided to take into his own home the eldest of the bewitched children the better to observe her, pray with her, and fight against the devil. The result of his researches was a book, *Memorable Providences Relating to Witchcraft and Possession,* published in 1689. The book contained a preface signed by four other Boston ministers;

their point was that this work laid to rest all doubts as to the reality of witchcraft.

> Men [they wrote], abandoning both faith and reason, count it their wisdom to credit nothing but what they see and feel. How much this fond opinion hath gotten ground in this debauched age is awfully observable; and what a dangerous stroke it gives to settle men in atheism is not hard to discern. . . . God is therefore pleased, besides the witness borne to this truth in Sacred Writ, to suffer devils sometimes to do such things in the world as shall stop the mouths of gainsayers, and extort a confession from them.

Mather himself, having surveyed the evidence in his volume, concluded: "Witchcraft is a siding with hell against heaven and earth, and therefore a witch is not to be endured in either. . . . Nothing too vile can be said of, nothing too hard can be done to, such a horrible iniquity as witchcraft itself!"

What with the excitement attending the overthrow of Andros, and the granting of a new charter in 1691, there was a pause in witch-hunting until early in 1692. Then three girls living with the family of the Rev. Mr. Parris of Salem Village (now Danvers) exhibited signs of having been bewitched. The Salem hunt was on and in one year in that village and others of Essex County, 20 witches (men and women) were executed, 50 others had confessed, 150 were in prison and another 200 had been accused.

Investigating committees sprang up; informers appeared; detailed descriptions of secret meetings of witches were forthcoming from those who had seen the light—and through it all appeared with special clarity the vengefulness of the Lord, the reality of the devil, the manifest need for the guidance of the ecclesiastical oligarchy.

But the hunt collapsed. It collapsed because the oligarchy was on its way out; because the economy was increasingly commercialized and the society increasingly heterogenous; because the new charter had secularized the government; because persecution for conscience's sake was being more and more widely questioned and the world outside more and more generally practiced some form of toleration.

But the *way* it was broken was through resistance. The courage and nobility of many of the martyrs and the prisoners impressed many; while the despicable nature and role of the informers disgusted many. The flimsiness of the evidence; its contradictory nature; its dependence upon admitted agents of the devil, began to bring the whole matter into doubt—and there were some who openly proclaimed not only their doubts as to the guilt of the particular prisoners but as to the very existence of witches.

The merchant enemies of the ecclesiastical oligarchy were particularly prominent in articulating the doubts—notably Thomas Brattle and Robert Clef. Ministers outside the areas dominated by the Mathers—like the pro-democratic Reverend John Wise of Ipswich, who had gone to prison in 1688 because of his leadership in the struggle against the Andros tyranny—began to cry out against the bloodspilling. While these did not question the reality of agents of the devil, they offered the idea that these agents might well be the unwilling and unwitting and entirely innocent victims of his guile, and that therefore they should not be punished.

It is important to note that these ideas were receiving wider and wider popular support—most of the scores of those arrested and punished were of the poor and the terror generally fell with greatest impact upon the poor. Thus, for example, petitions in defense of two of the "witches" (subsequently executed) were signed by over 50 people. That was a respectable total when the sparseness of the population of the 17th century Massachusetts is remembered and when it is borne in mind that each signer stood in danger of himself being accused of deviltry. Other collective petitions, as one signed by 24 residents of Andover, began to reach the authorities, denouncing the informers themselves as incredible witnesses and as "distempered persons." Then, grand juries began to refuse to indict and juries began to acquit, despite the fact that a presiding judge resigned in disgust in one case because the jury insisted on acquittal notwithstanding the perfect evidence of "guilt." And, as a final blow, some of the informers themselves began to retract. Soon this became epidemic and groups of three and eight of these tormented people would insist on regaining their humanity by making a clean breast of their vile lies. Within one year the hanging of witches stopped.

In this way the terror ceased—public opinion and public pressure forced it to stop—this despite the fact that as late as 1695 the Reverend Increase Mather, president of Harvard, sent out a circular to all Massachusetts ministers appealing to them to submit evidences of the impact of the invisible world and of the existence of witches. For ten years more he kept collecting such "evidences."

Chapter IX

Wise, "The Awakening" and Zenger

THE WITCHHUNTING CAMPAIGN was an act of desperation, as we have stated, by a declining ruling élite. It failed, after causing terrible tragedy and taking many lives. Its failure served as a boomerang to its initiators and helped push forward the elimination of the theological tyranny in Massachusetts.

I

In a further effort to regain their waning power, the leading Boston ministers began in the 1690's to question the congregationalist organization of their church. That which had been a fundament of their Puritan movement, now, in the declining days of the oligarchy, became increasingly insufferable. The Mathers and others began to urge a presbyterian type of organization, that is, one in which the autonomy of each congregation would be diluted, in which there would be established a closer union of the churches and a greater control of the individual churches by a ministerial association—the latter, obviously, dominated by the Boston elite.

Here the essence of original Puritanism was turned to good account to help destroy the Puritan oligarchy. This was occurring not only organizationally—in terms of congregationalism versus presbyterianism—but also, of course, ideologically. Thus, it was original Puritan doctrine that God had made man reasonable and that He had intended man to use that reason in pursuing truth—a critical doctrine with obvious overtones of danger to any authoritarian group, and one which favored natural, rather than revealed religion.

Again, the religious covenant idea of Puritanism was obviously applicable to the social scene. If the Lord sought men's consent before demanding that they obey His laws, surely no temporal ruler could demand unthinking and unconditional submission to his will. Moreover, if that God-given reason found the temporal ruler's will to be unreasonable—*i.e.*, unjust—then, naturally, the ruler's will was not to be obeyed. Here again was doctrine that easily could be turned against tyrannical and oppressive conduct.

The crystallizing of these contradictions occurred with the "Sixteen Proposals" of the leading Boston ministers in 1705 for the purposes of combining the churches of the Province and subordinating them to the control of the ministers' association. This evoked widespread discussion and popular opposition, the leadership of which once again was assumed by the Reverend John Wise of Ipswich.

This man, the son of an indentured servant, had become a popular hero with his defiance of the arbitrary taxation policy instituted by Governor Andros in the late 1680's. Arrested because he "did particularly excite and stir up His Majesty's subjects to refractoriness and disobedience—contrary to and in high contempt of His Majesty's laws and government here established," he had told the Governor's minions that this was not his offense, but that, rather: "We too boldly endeavored to persuade ourselves we were Englishmen and under privileges."

Wise was jailed and bail was refused him. A packed jury convicted him, after being subtly charged in these words by the judge: "I am glad there be so many worthy gentlemen of the jury so capable to do the King service and we expect a good verdict from you seeing the matter hath been so sufficiently proved against the criminal."

Wise tasted jail for several weeks, and suffered a heavy fine (plus heavier court costs), but with the aid of his townspeople he was released from prison. Though barred from his pulpit for one month he thereafter returned to the ministrations of neighbors who loved him—and after the overthrow of Andros, the town fully reimbursed the Reverend John Wise.

The "Sixteen Proposals" were widely debated and chewed over and Wise did not attempt to put his answer in print until 1710. His book, written in the form of a satire, was entitled *Churches Quarrel Espoused* and made the point that the full autonomy of the individual congregation had been a salient feature of Puritanism and had been reaffirmed as recently as the Synod of 1662. It insisted that this was most in accordance with deeply-felt and honestly-held religious convictions and that therefore presbyterianism should be rejected.

The book was widely read and a second edition was issued in 1715. This was followed, two years later, by a better volume on the same theme, entitled *A Vindication of the Government of New England Churches.* Here Wise propounded a political defense of religious independence and autonomy. Wise held government to be man-made and therefore subject to alteration by man; he held the end of government to be man's welfare. Wise held freedom to be natural and that government should constrain freedom as little as was consistent with social peace; he held that there was an essential dignity in man—in all men, of all rank and degree, and therefore a natural equality among all men. Thus, he felt Peter's injunction—"Honor all men"—to be a way to assure a just and peaceful social order.

Then Wise proceeded in classical vein to examine each of three possible forms of government—absolute monarchy, oligarchy, democracy—and to arrive, quite non-classically, at the conclusion that of the three it was democracy that was the best. It was, he held, "a form of government which the light of nature does highly value, and often directs to as most agreeable to the just and natural prerogatives of human beings."

The democratic form permits the people to care for their own welfare and it is the people who are the real sovereigns. If a few rule, they will rule for their own benefit and for the ill of the many—and ingenious will be the rationalizations: "For what is it that cunning and learned men can't make the world swallow as an article of their creed if they are once invested with an uncontrollable power, and are to be the standing orators to mankind in matters of faith and obedience?"

The purpose of "all good government is to cultivate humanity, and promote the happiness of all, and the good of every man in all his rights, his life, liberty, estate, honor, etc., without injury or abuse done to any." Hence, the "vindication of the government of New England churches" lies exactly in their autonomy, and in the supreme power of each congregation to determine the character and the acts of its own church. Hence, too, we should reject the "Sixteen Proposals" of the Boston few and hold on to our autonomy.

The ideas of Wise were not only his own, and this is their greatest significance. They were the ideas of his congregation and of most of the folk of New England, who upheld Wise's position and rejected that of the very learned—and sorely threatened—hierarchy. Wise's writings had lasting impact and, reprinted in 1772, played a part in affirming a greater independence than the village church in Ipswich.[1]

II

The decisive blow to the Puritan oligarchy came with the Great Awakening, which left it shattered both ideologically and institutionally. But that was only one of the results of this tremendous phenomenon that swept Britain and all of her colonies for about 50 years beginning in the 1720's.

The movement cut across sectarian lines, encompassing Calvinists like Jonathan Edwards of Massachusetts and George Whitefield in England, Church of England repudiators of Calvin like Charles and John Wesley, Theodore Frelinghuysen of the Dutch Reformed church in New Jersey and Gilbert Tennent and Samuel Davies of the Presbyterian in New Jersey and in Virginia. Its impact was felt in America from Connecticut to the Carolinas.

Despite great differences there were certain common attributes to the Great Awakening. It was, first of all, a mass movement, and preachers like John Wesley and George Whitefield spoke in the open fields to tens of thousands of workers and miners and farmers, to servants and even to slaves. It was, secondly, a movement of salvation for the common man and it was one in which he could *participate;* it pulsated equality and concern for the saving of all. It made of religion a deeply personal experience, yet one to be collectively expressed; it challenged the élite and the erudite.

At the same time, much of it was fundamentalist, in protest against the Deism that was becoming increasingly fashionable among the well-to-do in particular. Yet, this is mixed, for there are evidences that agnosticism and even atheism had begun to penetrate among the poor and to cause concern to the guardians of the status quo. Even the very liberal Benjamin Franklin, himself a Deist by the 1730's, warned that "talking against religion is unchaining a tiger; the beast let loose may worry his liberator." It must be remembered, too, that the crowded cities of England with the closely-packed masses of miserably exploited were becoming a fearful police problem for the ruling class, and fervent revivalism, with a dash of social reformism, might well be helpful.

In the American colonies, while some of the Awakening takes the form of attacking learning per se (because the learned were the rich and those in charge of state and church)—very much as some of the earliest proletarians seek to destroy the machines, rather than take control of them—its main content is socially and intellectually invigorating and emancipating. And the class lines in the Awakening were clear and closely associated with developing political clashes and polarizations.

"The vulgar everywhere are inclined to enthusiasm," remarked one of the "Old Light" clergymen. The upstarts were "men of all occupations . . . young persons . . . women and girls; yea, Negroes, have taken upon them to do the business of preachers." In Connecticut, the General Association of Ministers warned that the "awakened" were "chiefly of the lower and younger sort." These were "murmurers and complainers . . . despising government"; they were "fierce and wrathful" people, who dared to criticize "their rulers and teachers," the "magistrates and principal gentlemen."

Charges of blasphemy and of subversion abounded and many were the ministers fired, the students expelled, the partisans fined and jailed. And in all the colonies there was an organic connection between the development of popular parties that took the lead against British restrictions and Anglican Church pretensions and against the conservative parties in local politics.

The Great Awakening broke altogether the ascendancy of the old established churches and brought into being a popular religion. It invigorated democratic conduct and thought and stimulated equalitarian ideas, including ideas hostile to slavery and even, in some cases, to racism.

It created, in its great meetings and in its institutional results —especially the building of the Methodist and Baptist churches —something approximating bona-fide popular collective organizations. It led to the multiplying of educational efforts, despite something of a bias against learning, and resulted in the founding, for example, of Dutch-Reformed Rutgers, Presbyterian Princeton, Baptist Brown and Congregationalist Dartmouth. And by being an inter-colonial movement of really popular dimensions, it did much to undermine provincialism in the colonies and to develop a sense of unity—of oneness, of American nationality.

III

The art of printing makes possible a great enhancement in the power of public opinion; hence tyrants have always looked askance at the press. Could they have prevented its discovery they would have done so; being faced with an accomplished fact, oppressive ruling classes thought first of making the new machine useful by forbidding any but its licensed agents to employ it. When this could no longer be retained, the rulers moved on to strict censorship and to sedition and criminal libel laws holding printers accountable for whatever disturbing matter —true or not—might appear in their publications.

In the 17th century, English law had a very rigid conception of what might indeed be disturbing. In fact, the only really safe course was for the printer to have no discussion of any kind concerning politics or governmental affairs in his paper. Thus, in 1679, when one Henry Carr was on trial for some material in a weekly paper, the Chief Justice declared it criminal under common law, to "write on the subject of government, whether in terms of praise or censure, it is not material; for no man has a right to say anything of government."

Yet this gave way rather quickly to making criminal the printing of anything held to be critical of government or governors. Thus it was that the first newspaper to appear in English America—the *Boston Public Occurrences,* published in 1690 by Benjamin Harris—lasted only one issue, for that issue was critical of the government's conduct of a then current war and government forbade its continuance.

The first colonial newspaper that lasted any period of time was the *Boston News-Letter* which appeared in 1704. While most of the colonial newspapers were more or less official organs of the ruling cliques and so continued undisturbed by the law, of several this was not true.

Generally speaking, in fact, the newspapers were especially consequential to merchants, lawyers and other professional people, containing news pertinent to their businesses, and as these classes became more and more inhibited by English colonialism the papers became more and more controversial. Indeed, as class stratification appeared and as the colonial economy matured, the papers became more and more identified with the resulting political parties and groups.

In Massachusetts, as we have seen, the merchants and others became increasingly bold in their hostility to the theocracy as the 17th century faded away and the next began. Blow after blow was dealt this ruling clique and finally within Boston itself the opposition became bold enough, in 1721, to issue its own newspaper—the *New England Courant,* edited by James Franklin, elder half-brother of Benjamin.

The Boston authorities became restive under the attacks of this paper, especially as these began to attract letters from readers expressing agreement. Within a year Cotton Mather was confiding to his diary that:

> Warnings are to be given unto the wicked printer, and his accomplices, who every week publish a vile paper to lessen and blacken the Ministers of the town, and render their ministry ineffectual. A wickedness never parall'd anywhere upon the face of the earth.

In 1722, James Franklin was arrested for promoting sedition, held in jail for several weeks, and then released under bond. But his paper continued to give offense to the authorities and, in 1723, they ordered him to cease its publication. James Franklin refused to honor this order, and the sheriff was directed to apprehend him. Meanwhile, for two weeks, the *New England Courant* appeared with the name of young Benjamin Franklin as the printer, thus technically conforming to the authorities' order.

When James Franklin ended his brief period as a hunted political fugitive, an effort was made to get the Grand Jury to indict him for sedition, but that body refused. Hence the prosecution ceased and the *New England Courant* continued publication for several more years.

IV

Ten years after the harassment of James Franklin, occurred an even more consequential case, that of another poor printer, the German immigrant, John Peter Zenger of New York City. This again reflects the developing political battles within the colonies.

The Zenger case arose out of the rising opposition of merchants, lawyers, artisans and mechanics in the growing metropolis of New York City (with a population then of about 10,000, of whom some 1,700 were Negro slaves) to the domination of the province by large landholders. It was precipitated by the following events.

In July, 1731, Governor Montgomerie of the Province died, and he was succeeded, as acting governor, by the senior councillor, a prosperous merchant, Rip Van Dam. Van Dam held this position for 13 months until the arrival of the Royal Governor, one William Cosby.

This Cosby typified the British colonial governor at his worst. Son of a wealthy absentee Irish landlord, and himself a Colonel of the Royal Irish Regiment, Cosby had recently been removed as Governor of the island of Minorca because of particularly gross mishandling of funds and extraordinary unpopularity. He was an avaricious, coarse and brutal official.

One of his earliest actions was to express disdain for the meagre monetary gift the New York Assembly voted him; his second was to seize half the salary of Van Dam as acting governor and to demand that the rest be turned over to him. This Van Dam refused to do.

Governor Cosby set up a special court of equity for the specific purpose of suing Van Dam. This arbitrary act directed at the senior officer of the local officialdom infuriated the Assembly and solidified opposition within the City to the Governor.

The Chief Justice of the Province, Lewis Morris, refused to serve on the newly-created court; for this his integrity as a jurist was directly impugned by Cosby, and when the imputation was as publicly resented, the Governor removed Morris from the bench, after 18 years as Chief Justice. The leading attorney of the City, James Alexander, joined Van Dam as his lawyer and forced the Governor to drop his utterly illegal course—not before, however, that official had actually declared Van Dam in rebellion and had tried, without success, to sequester all his funds.

Meanwhile, Cosby attempted to deal the merchant party a blow by disfranchising all Quakers, since he insisted that affirmation alone would not be sufficient for the exercise of the suffrage. He followed this with active gobbling of graft such as rivaled that of such governor-thieves as Fletcher and Cornbury; and with very generous land grants made out to himself.

A result of this was the consolidation of an opposition political party, the Popular Party, and the establishment of a newspaper (there had been up to then but one newspaper, and it was issued by the public printer and so was an organ of the Governor and the landlords) to serve as the voice of this opposition. That paper was the *New York Weekly Journal,* launched in November, 1733, and its printer was John Peter Zenger; its chief aim, said James Alexander, was "chiefly to expose him"—meaning Governor Cosby.

The new paper at once exceeded the circulation of the old, and was forced frequently to issue several editions and to print special supplements. The popularity came from the hatred of the governor and the vigor of its prose—contributed by figures like Lewis Morris, James Alexander, Cadwallader Colden, William Smith and other outstanding members of the colonial bourgeoisie. Typical was this explanation of its purpose:

> Some have said it is not the businesss of private men to meddle with government. . . . Since it is the great design of this paper to maintain and explain the glorious Principles of Liberty, and to expose the arts of those who would darken or destroy them, I shall here particularly show the wickedness and stupidity of the above saying. . . . To say that private men have nothing to do with government is to say that private men have nothing to do with their own happiness and misery.

The paper continued a drumfire of attacks upon tyranny and corruption; it featured exposures that did everything but name the names that—since they were universally known—did not need naming. It was the mainstay of the city elections of 1734, in which the tyranny and corruption of Cosby were the central issues. On the streets appeared broadside letters from mechanics and artisans, signed "Timothy Wheelwright" and "John Chisel" denouncing oppression and calling for an assertion of "ancient liberties." Other leaflets appeared with ballads set to popular tunes, with such stanzas as:

> *To you good lads that dare oppose*
> *All lawless power and might*
> *You are the theme that we have chose,*
> *And to your praise we write*

and

> *Tho' pettyfogging knaves deny*
> *Us rights of Englishmen;*
> *We'll make the scoundrel rascals fly,*
> *And ne'er return again*

The Popular Party won a resounding victory in the city election. The Governor demanded that the common hangman burn the offending ballads, but the grand jury refused to return such an order. The Governor then sought to force the Assembly to agree to the indictment of John Peter Zenger, but that body refused. The Governor sought to get the Grand Jury to indict Zenger for seditious libel, but he failed here, too; whereupon Zenger was arrested on the basis of an "information" returned against him by the Provincial Council.

So in this extraordinary manner—on the basis of a warrant issued by the Council, though its power to issue such a warrant was highly dubious, and without citing evidence of crime and without opportunity to offer defense—the printer was apprehended on November 17, 1734, "for publishing several seditious libels . . . having in them many things tending to raise factions and tumults, among the people."

For one week Zenger was closely confined and permitted neither to see nor to communicate with anyone whatsoever. Bail was set at £400, which, said Zenger, was exactly ten times more than all his earthly possessions. The printer remained in jail.

After the first week, Zenger's wife was permitted to converse with him through the grating of his cell door and in this way that remarkable man and his remarkable wife managed to get out a newspaper throughout the months of his confinement and trial.

James Alexander and William Smith stepped forward as attorneys for Zenger. They attempted to press exceptions to the holding of Zenger in jail on the basis of the unusual mode by which he was apprehended, as explained above, but their arguments were rejected by the Chief Justice, newly appointed by Cosby. When Smith and Alexander pressed their case with vigor bothersome to His Honor, this worthy found them in contempt and excluded them from the bar, and appointed as Zenger's attorney one John Chambers, a nonentity serving the Governor's political party.

Alexander and Morris took their disbarment to the Assembly and while they did not get immediate relief they did make some extremely telling and—alas! still highly pertinent—remarks.

> That we were perfectly innocent, and did our duty in the case of Zenger, is what we have the clearest sense of. . . . Had we err'd, must a man lose his livelihood for an innocent mistake? Must his brains be beat out, because they are not cast in the same mould with another man's? . . . If these things are to be tolerated . . . hard will be the case of lawyers, who are sworn to use their offices according to their learning and discretion. Yet, by this rule, we must not be permitted to use either. Instead of consulting our law books, and doing what we think consistent therewith, for the benefit of our clients, we must study in great men's causes, only what will please the judges, and what will most flatter men in power.

The popular party refused to accept the court-appointed lawyer and sought high and low, within and outside New York, for an attorney with sufficient learning and reputation and courage to make a real fight of the case. Lawyer after lawyer rejected all requests. Finally, the most distinguished attorney in the colonies, approaching his 80th birthday, accepted the challenge. This was Andrew Hamilton (no relation to the future statesman) of Philadelphia, who had been attorney general of

Pennsylvania from 1717 to 1726, a Vice Admiralty Judge, and Speaker of the Pennsylvania Assembly from 1729 to 1739. Despite the infirmities of age and illness, Hamilton made the arduous trip to New York City and entered the case of the printer Zenger and thus, too, the company of immortal fighters for human freedom.

The formal charge against the prisoner when the court convened—in the City Hall, at the corner of present Nassau and Wall Streets, on August 4, 1735, with the room crammed with spectators—was "printing and publishing a false, scandalous and seditious libel, in which his Excellency the Governor of this Province, who is the King's immediate representative here, is greatly and unjustly scandalized."

Hamilton concentrated his fire on the word "false" in the charge and argued—against then established law—that in bringing forth a defense he could properly seek to show that what had been published had not been false. The court rejected this argument for, as the Government attorney immediately pointed out, "the law says their being true is an aggravation of the crime."

Well, then, said Hamilton, if I may not be allowed to prove them true, will the government be required to prove them "false" as charged? Certainly not, said the Judge, and he added, for the edification of the jury: "It was a very great offense to speak evil, or to revile, those in authority over us." That, said the judge, was the law.

Well, argued Hamilton, law changes. At one time in English history, he said, men had been punished for declaring that the tyranny of a King might be resisted; today, since our Glorious Revolution, a man may be punished for insisting that a King's tyranny may NOT be resisted.

Moreover, argued Hamilton, what may be law for England, need not be law for America; and, at any rate, that which is applicable to His Majesty personally in England, need not be applicable to a mere servant of that Personage, thousands of miles away.

Hamilton then turned to the jury and appealed to its members to keep truth in their minds, and to remember that the reason for a jury—men selected from the neighborhood—was presumably that they will be able to judge of the truth, especially as that truth is comprehended within the area of the alleged crime. The Court insisted that the jury had nothing to do with the truth or falsehood of the charges and that this was in no way relevant to the case. But, said Hamilton, does not the crime of libel depend upon understanding—to be found guilty of libel must not one be *understood* as being libelous and are not the jury members the ones to say whether or not they *understand* what the defendant published to be or not to be libelous?

The Court repeated its negative and said the jury must decide only whether or not the defendant had published the material in question; but, said Hamilton, this we have admitted and if this alone were indeed the question the proceedings here would be farcical. The jury can confine itself, if it wishes, to the limits set by Your Honor; but, Hamilton insisted to the jury, it *need* not do so—it could, if it wished, examine the essence of the matter, the *subject* of the complaint, and on this basis render a verdict as to whether or not John Peter Zenger was guilty of the crime of seditious libel.

Having established this as his case, despite repeated interruption from the court and its adverse rulings, Hamilton proceeded to his argument. There is no better way to present this argument—short of full quotation, which space forbids—than by allowing Hamilton to speak for himself where he develops his salient points:

> The high things that are said in favor of rulers, and of their dignities, and upon the side of power, will not be able to stop people's mouths when they feel themselves oppressed, I mean in a free government.
> There is heresy in law, as well as in religion, and both have changed very much; and we well know that it is not two centuries ago that a man would have been burnt as a heretic, for owning such opinions in matters of religion, as are publicly wrote and printed at this day. They were fallible men, it seems, and we take the liberty not only to differ from them in religious

opinion, but to condemn them and their opinions too. . . . In New-York a man may make free with his God, but he must take special care what he says of his governor.

Who, that is the least acquainted with history or law, can be ignorant of the specious pretences, which have often been made use of by men in power, to introduce arbitrary rule, and destroy the liberties of a free people . . . it is a duty which all good men owe to their country, to guard against the unhappy influences of ill men when intrusted with power, and especially against their creatures and dependents, who, as they are generally more necessitous, are surely more covetous and cruel.

Men who injure and oppress the people under their administration provoke them to cry out and complain; and then make that very complaint the foundation for new oppressions and prosecutions.

Clearly, then, Hamilton knew the case to be a purely political one; he knew the political temper of the mass of the people of New York. Hence, did he develop his case in this completely political and non-technical manner. He closed his appeal to the jury on the same note and in doing so came perilously close himself to "libeling" the distinguished Governor.

The question before the Court and you, gentlemen of the jury, is not of small nor private concern, it is not the cause of a poor printer, nor of New-York alone, which you are now trying. No! it may in its consequence, affect every freeman that lives under a British government in America. It is the best cause. It is the cause of liberty . . . of exposing and opposing arbitrary power (in these parts of the world at least) by speaking and writing truth.

The Government reiterated its insistence that Mr. Hamilton's arguments were quite irrelevant to the case at hand, and urged the jury to bring in the only verdict it could—in the light of the admission by the defendent that he was indeed the printer of the passages in question—namely, a verdict of guilty. In doing this the jury would be upholding law and order, the dignity of the Crown and the peaceableness of His Majesty's benign administration in our own New York.

The jury withdrew and in a short time announced that it had reached a verdict. The clerk faced the foreman, Thomas Hunt, and asked "whether John Peter Zenger was guilty of printing and publishing the libels in the information mentioned?" The foreman answered at once: "Not Guilty"; upon which says a contemporary record, "there were three Huzzas in the hall which was crowded with people."

When Hamilton left for Philadelphia the next day, the guns of every merchant ship in the harbor fired a salute, and in September, 1735, the Common Council of New York presented him with the freedom of the city. Zenger, himself, was made the public printer for the colony of New York in 1737.

The trial had been followed with intense interest throughout the English colonies and in Britain and all Europe. Zenger printed the trial record in 1736 and it sold very widely. Thereafter four editions of the trial proceedings were printed in England, one in Boston and another in Lancaster, Pennsylvania. The Zenger edition was again reprinted in 1770 in New York, as part of the revolutionary upsurge, just as the writings of John Wise, as we have seen, were reprinted in the 1770's.

Andrew Hamilton was quite correct, of course, in his estimate of the historic meaning a verdict of acquittal would have. It established the precedent for the principle that in prosecution for libel the jury was to judge of both law and facts—*i.e.,* that truth was a plea effective against the charge of libel. The momentous relationship of this to the struggle for freedom of speech and press and for the whole democratic effort against tyranny is manifest.

Of course, while the Zenger case was a precedent, it did not, of itself, establish this reading of the law. On the contrary, it took several more generations until the change became accepted. It was only in 1784 that the preeminent English barrister, Sir Thomas Erskine, used the Hamilton argument successfully in a libel case; the principle was put into law by Parliament in 1792 —and even later in most of the United States.

V

A noteworthy fact, deserving particular comment, is that the religiously and politically heretical and schismatic enterprises which are so large a part of colonial history—Roger Williams, Anne Hutchinson and John Wise, witches, Quakers and "New Lighters," and seditionists like Zenger—found widespread public encouragement and numerous adherents or sympathizers, despite the heavy penalties involved.[2]

In this connection, Professor Rossiter is quite wrong, though in agreement with the view expressed in most historical writing on the subject, when he declares, in the introduction to his *Seedtime of the Republic,* that it is "the preachers, merchants, planters, and lawyers who were the mind of colonial America." They were the literate body, on the whole, of that society, but the masses of slaves and servants and laborers and artisans and mechanics and yeomen also had minds, filled with ideas, and ideas that were frequently different from those of their "betters." Their ideas found expression in activities other than bookmaking, usually, but were not the less real for that. And what is more, as the careers of such as Williams and Hutchinson and Wise and Zenger show, they found expression, too, in support, if not at times in inspiration, for the forward-looking ideas enunciated by the subversive intelligentsia of the period.

Chapter X

A New Nationality in a New World

THE COLONIAL PERIOD culminated in a national revolution. Manifestly the prerequisite for such a revolution was the existence of a nationality, and in this case the new nationality asserting its right to self-determination was the American.

To this day, however, distinguished thinkers, including American thinkers, are of the opinion that the United States is not a nation. Professor John Herman Randall, for example, contributing a paper on "The Spirit of American Philosophy" to a collective work entitled *Wellsprings of the American Spirit* (1948) insists that the United States "is a continent and not a nation" and that, therefore, regional and sectional differences and conflicts have been "the very substance of our history," rather than some national fabric whose weaving can be traced and whose pattern can be discerned.

Those who think this way are in error, I believe, and are confusing complexities and specifics and variations with substantive differences, though it is true that sectional differences have been particularly important in U. S. history. Not only does the United States form a nation in the mid-twentieth century; the thirteen colonies had laid the groundwork for nationhood by the mid-eighteenth century and, with 20 addi-

tional years of maturation, were able to unite and make good
their claim to nationhood on the field of battle.

I

The forging of the American nationality was based upon two
centuries of common and unique experiences; it was the creation of two centuries of togetherness; of the conquest of nature;
of contiguity here and vast separation from Europe; of new
fauna and flora and climate; of the Indian challenge; of the
colonial status and the developing resistance to that status; of
the continuing conquest of the wilderness, which in turn moved
many of the Americans—and this was their separate and
common title by the end of the 17th century—even further away
from Europe and made them more intent on problems and
conditions peculiar to themselves.

The process of estrangement from England was a dialectical
one; it was not only that the Americans felt a oneness among themselves stemming from their remoteness from England; it was
further the fact that the English in turn thought of America
almost as of another planet. People like Boswell and Johnson
confessed to each other late in the 1760's that they knew
nothing of America, and Johnson showed his ignorance by
declaring that America was a home of "barbarism." Even
Englishmen professionally concerned with America were woe-
fully ignorant of the New World. Thus, the Board of Trade,
chief colonial administrative organ, confused its deliberations at
various times by such errors as thinking that Perth Amboy was
in the West Indies rather than in New Jersey, or that Virginia
was an island, or that the Indians confederated as the Six
Nations resided in the West Indies. Indeed, commonly the
thirteen colonies were thought of in England as part of the West
Indies, and a geography textbook[1] published by the Oxford
University Press, and, as its subtitle said, "designed for the use
of young students in the universities," contained a chapter
entitled "Of America or the West Indies."

It is no wonder that the colonies continually felt the need for more or less permanently-stationed agents in England, so that by the 1760's one such like Benjamin Franklin had acquired many of the characteristics of an Ambassador from one country to another.

Knowledge of the fundamental divergence in interest between the colonists themselves and the British rulers dominating the colonies led very early to suspicions and premonitions and fears that, with development, the colonists would wrench themselves free and assert their independence. James Harrington, in his very influential *Commonwealth of Oceana,* published in 1656, commented that the American colonies "are yet babes that cannot live without sucking the breasts of their mother cities, but such as I mistake if, when they come of age, they do not wean themselves."

Thereafter the same idea, and even image, recurs in English literature. Thus, a 1707 pamphlet by the distinguished botanist, Nehemiah Grew, warned that "when the colonies may become populous and, with the increase of arts and sciences, strong," they then, "forgetting their relation to the mother country [may] confederate and consider nothing further than the means to support their ambition of standing on their legs." Again, one of the widely-read *Cato's Letters* of 1722, observed: "No creatures suck the teats of their dam longer than they can draw milk from thence. . . . Nor will any country continue their subjection to another, only because their great grandmothers were acquainted."

Samuel Johnson, writing in the *Literary Magazine* in 1756, commented on "the fear that the American colonies will break off their dependence on England," though he went on to show his own ignorance by dismissing the fear as "chimerical and vain."

Oliver Goldsmith, in *The Citizen of the World* (1762) warned that the colonies were growing so populous and so powerful that their continued subordination to England was unlikely, for: "The colonies should always bear an exact proportion to the mother country; when they grow populous, they grow powerful, and by becoming powerful, they become independent also; thus subordination is destroyed." Similarly, a Frenchman, visiting the colonies in 1765, already wrote of them as of a unit and was sure that "this country cannot be long subject to Great Britain, nor indeed to any distant power." He thought this was evident, for "its extent is so great, the daily increase of its inhabitants so considerable, and having everything within themselves for more than their own defence, that no nation whatsoever seems better calculated for independency."

Two years later, Benjamin Franklin in England was writing along similar lines to Lord Kames. In this letter one also clearly detects sharp national feeling in the bitter denunciation of English arrogance relative to the colonies and in the evident pride with which the attributes of the native land were touched upon.

> Every man in England seems to consider himself a piece of a sovereign over America [wrote Franklin]; seems to jostle himself into the throne with the King, and talks of *our subjects* in the colonies. . . . But America, an immense territory, favored by nature with all the advantages of climate, soils, great navigable rivers, lakes, etc., must become a great country, populous and mighty; and will, in a less time than is general conceived, be able to shake off any shackles that may be imposed upon her, and perhaps place them on the imposers.

Indeed, back in 1755, 20-year-old John Adams wrote a friend that perhaps the "great seat of empire" would yet move to America. "It looks likely to me," he said, once we can get rid of the French threat, for clearly "our people . . . in another century [will] become more numerous than England itself. Should this be the case," he continued, "since we have, I may say, all the naval stores of the nation in our hands, it will be easy to obtain the mastery of the seas; and then the united force of all Europe will not be able to subdue us." Young Adams went on, in this remarkable letter: "The only way to keep us from setting up for ourselves is to disunite us. *Divide et impera.* Keep us in distinct colonies. . . ."

This was exactly the prescription of the most knowing of British colonial administrators. Thus, Thomas Pownall, who in the 1750's was secretary to the New York Governor and himself governor of Massachusetts and then of South Carolina, insisted in his basic work, *The Administration of the Colonies* (1764), that it was "essential to the preservation of the empire to keep them [the colonies] disconnected and independent of each other."

II

At the same time, problems of administration drove the English authorities repeatedly towards efforts at unifying the colonial governmental apparatus. This was attempted in order to curtail local autonomy, which tended to encourage separatism and lax law enforcement, and in a frank effort to dominate the colonies, more economically and effectively. The attempts go back to the 17th century—notably the effort at confederation under Andros —and continue on to at least the Albany Congress of 1754, where, however, evidence of more colonial initiative is present.

A whole complex of motives and feelings were interwoven. The colonists tended to reject any effort at consolidation which seemed English-motivated for fear that tighter centralization would mean greater tyranny. At the same time common interests were knitting the colonists together and suggestions of institutional unity reappear (outstanding is Benjamin Franklin in this regard) but here the British, while seeming to favor and to urge centralization, would display hostility. In all cases it is the substance and not the form which is decisive.

Throughout colonial history, while there is intercolonial jealousy, there is also a persistent drive towards unity and cooperation, a manifestation, as it is a source, of growing nationality. This is especially true, as we have seen earlier, in mass revolutionary and insurrectionary colonial movements. It is so striking that Charles M. Andrews in the introduction to his invaluable collection, *Narratives of the Insurrections,* commented: "One

cannot study the insurrections as a whole without noticing the
mutual dependence of one colony upon another." Thus, in the
North Carolina (Albemarle) turmoil, New Englanders played
a part; in Bacon's effort, men from North Carolina were
present; in all the manifestations of unrest in Virginia and in
Maryland there was joint activity; the Leisler rebellion provoked
correspondence and interchange with inhabitants of Massachusetts, Maryland and Connecticut; and it was Boston sympathizers of Leisler who prevailed on Parliament to remove his
attainder.

With colonial growth came not only a developing sense of
self-sufficiency, but also of interdependence. Roads appeared
knitting together the colonies, and by 1739, good post-roads ran
from Portsmouth, New Hampshire, to Charleston, South Carolina. There was much inter-visiting and even inter-marriage;
there was, too, much moving, so that it was not at all unusual
for one family to have resided during a single decade in two
or even three different colonies, and yet feel themselves inhabitants of something that was indeed unitary, that was American.

Beginning with Harvard in 1636 and William and Mary in
1693, colleges patterned after those in England sprang up
throughout the colonies, but because of conditions peculiar to
their locale, "by the middle of the eighteenth century," writes
Richard Hofstadter, "there had emerged an American system
of collegiate education different not only from the English
models with which Americans were most familiar but from all
others as well." [2]

And by that period there were several colleges other than the
two pioneers, including Yale (1701), Princeton (1746), King's
(1754, later Columbia), Philadelphia (1755, later the University of Pennsylvania), Brown (1764), Queen's (1766, later
Rutgers), and Dartmouth (1769). To each of these institutions
came students not only from the immediate vicinity but from
neighboring and even distant colonies, so that the rising American professional groups had had from their earliest training a
more than local background.

Professional and cultural organizations were founded reflecting the same growing nationality, such as the *American* Philosophical Society and the *American* Medical Society, both of which had active members, who corresponded and visited with each other, scattered from Georgia to New England.[3]

III

It must be remembered, too, that the newness of America came not only from the fact that it was new—the New World—but also from the fact, and this was implicit in the idea of its being a New World, that many came here with the deliberate intent of creating something new as compared to conditions in Europe. It was not only a matter of starting over again, or seeking one's fortune, which were important enough. It was also a matter of conscious planning and organization, a matter of deliberately seeking to build a different way of life, as was true, for instance, of the founders of Massachusetts, Rhode Island, Pennsylvania, and Georgia.

And even old things took on new meanings and new characters here, because they were here. Thus, an Anglican Church was established in certain of the colonies, but in none was there a Bishop and though London wanted an American Bishopric, the colonists did not want it and did not get it. This reflected the greater independence and autonomy of the Anglican church in the colonies as compared with the "same" church in England. And the vestries, in Virginia especially, were quite different from and more powerful than analogous organizations in the old country.

In the New World, as in England, ownership of land was generally required for one to be a voter, but this was, in fact, very much more restrictive in England than it was in the colonies, a difference with enormous impact upon the character of politics here as compared with there. Similarly, with compactness something sought after and with neighborliness a necessity of survival in the New World, there never developed here any-

thing like "virtual" representation in various governing bodies—
a commonplace in England. Here an area was spoken for by
one who inhabited that area and this became a fixture in
American politics, quite unlike the pattern in England.

Moreover, in the colonies with land so abundant, it was
common not to pass it on in its entirety to the eldest son, even if
the landowner died without a will. This was not true throughout the colonies—Virginia, for instance, had primogeniture—
but it was true in most of the colonies most of the time, and was
quite different from conditions in England.

IV

The general pattern of local life in the colonies, in addition to
the altered nature of the Virginia vestries, was different from
that in England and, generally speaking, tended to be more
democratic, more responsive to the actual will of many of the
residents. An outstanding example of this was the town meeting
institution of New England; it was so significant a feature of
colonial life, in one area, at any rate, and has had such lasting
impact on the development of local government in other areas
of the United States, particularly the mid-West, that it is worth
a closer examination.

Compactness was important in the New World as a matter
of survival, and congregational organization was basic to the
Puritan way. Colonists came over as a group, with entire
families arriving together. Accordingly, settlement in towns was
the original and basic mode by which the Massachusetts Bay
colony and other New England colonies were settled. In county
government, the New England pattern did not differ very much
from that of old England, but in town government it did. The
New England town governments, beginning in the 1630's, had
greater freedom and power in the handling of local affairs,
and greater influence in helping determine central government
policies than did their counterparts in England.

Generally speaking, too, as the movement against the theological oligarchy grew, the center of gravity for political power moved away from the church meeting to the town meeting. Furthermore, throughout the colonial years the tendency, *among the colonists,* was to expand the number of active participants in the town meetings and to enhance the powers of those meetings. As is to be expected, on the other hand, the English authorities always looked with suspicion on these town meetings as "nests of sedition" and from time to time sought to curb their rights.

The town meetings and the elections of town officers, especially the selectmen, became decisive political struggles—schools for the growth of rudimentary political parties and for the development of such formidable politicians as the Adamses, the Hancocks and the Otises. The very conscientious John Adams held many offices in a full and long life; none gave him more concern than that of selectman in Boston. In his diary, March 3, 1766, he remarked that his recent election had "brought upon me a multiplicity of new cares." He named four which are indicative of the wide powers of selectmen and the great local autonomy exercised by the New England town governments: education, providing for the poor, taxation, and road building and maintenance.

In New England it was the town which elected representatives to the General Court, or the assembly, and the quotas of the colonies' taxes were assessed upon each town, which then proceeded to realize the necessary total. On the other hand, in law the towns were basically subordinate to the colonial assembly and, ultimately, to the English authority; still, the development of local autonomy served to make of the town meetings instruments for defying that distant authority. While local power was more developed in New England than elsewhere, it is important to note that county governments in the middle colonies—New York and Pennsylvania, in particular—had greater powers and were more responsive to popular pressure than their counterparts in England.

V

With population sparse in the colonies it is noticeable that there was a general easing of the criminal code as compared with England, and fewer crimes were punishable by hanging. There was, too, a quicker development, in practice, of relative freedom of press and assemblage and of religion. With people coming from a score of different countries, practicing dozens of religions and no religion, with infinite variations in backgrounds and customs, the society simply could not survive unless it practiced co-existence. All this loosening of conventional bonds did not come of itself; it came rather through organized effort, but behind the success of such effort lay the altered objective conditions of life in the New World.

The mixing of peoples included those who were especially bitter toward England, as some from Scotland, but especially, of course, those from Ireland; tens of thousands of the latter came to the colonies during the pre-Revolutionary generation. In addition, *the* great attraction of America to the poor of Europe was that it offered the possibility of owning land—the basic test of status in Europe and the secret of independence. As the Scots said: "He who owns the land, owns the man"—and in spacious, unsettled America it appeared possible for all, if white, to own land.

Said Crevecoeur, a Frenchman living in Pennsylvania, writing in the 1770's, and discussing the question, What is an American?:

> In this great American asylum, the poor of Europe have by some means met together, and in consequence of various causes. To what purpose should they ask one another what countrymen they are? Alas, two-thirds of them had no country. Can a wretch, who wanders about, who works and starves, whose life is a continual scene of sore affliction or pinching penury; can that man call England or any other kingdom his country? A country that had no bread for him; whose fields procured him no harvest; who met with nothing but the frowns

of the rich, the severity of the laws, with jails and punishments; who owned not a single foot of the extensive surface of this planet?

Crevecoeur very much exaggerated the well-being of the mass of Americans, but it is a fact that more people were better off in the American colonies, proportionately, than was true of any land in Europe from whence they may have come. It is also true that there was a much higher percentage of land owners among the American population than among the English. It was the possibility of owning land that drove the colonists, once here, to constantly move westward; this not only further removed them psychologically and physically, from England, it also gave them a stake in this society and made them lovers of America, made them Americans.

VI

Meanwhile, the material development of the colonies proceeded. By 1770 while England and Wales had perhaps seven million inhabitants, the colonies had about two and a half millions. Class stratification was well developed in the colonies and a burgeoning economic system was in evidence. Well before the Revolution, textile production was not confined to local markets, nor was shoe and lumber production. Flour mills were reaching out to an intercolonial—and wider—market; and by 1775 the colonies produced more pig and bar iron than did England plus Wales.

At the same time, within the thirteen colonies, there appeared "a powerful stimulus to the evolution of a national economy," as one study puts it,[4] in the fact that by the 1760's, a uniformity had appeared in prices, commercial law, and business conditions and practices.

All these developments produced a unique history; a set of experiences and problems and struggles that were binding the colonists together, that were already producing the rudiments of those "mystic chords" that Lincoln was to conjure up a century hence. And all of them were colonists together of a single "mother" country, having, because of this, similar ties and problems and demands and restraints which helped mightily to produce a oneness.

And while England was the "mother" country for many colonists right down to the Revolution, nevertheless Englishmen were frequently classified as "foreigners" in the colonial press by about 1765.

VII

Giving voice to the common interests and helping to make them common and to create a consciousness of unity was a growing American culture. Newspapers appeared in every colony and some had audiences that crossed provincial boundaries. Magazines appeared, "for all the colonies" as one of them announced; in 1741 an *American Magazine* appeared in Philadelphia and in the same year and city, Franklin's *General Magazine*. Other *American* Magazines appeared—in Boston (1744), and again in Philadelphia (1757), the latter announcing in its first number that one of its main aims was "to give one colony an idea of the public state of another."

In these organs, and as separate publications, an American poetry made its appearance, culminating in Philip Freneau's "Poem on the Rising Glory of America," delivered at the 1771 commencement at Princeton. Here the poet, in seeing the rising glory of his homeland saw:

> . . . *a train, a glorious train appear,*
> *Of Patriots plac'd in equal fame with those*
> *Who nobly fell for Athens or for Rome.*

American artists like Robert Feke, Charles Peale, John Copley made their mark in the colonial period. They showed clear national features in their work and evoked an acclaim that can only be considered patriotic and national. Historians of the colonies came forward, living and writing and publishing in the colonies and treating of particular areas, as Byrd of Virginia,

Prince of New York and Hutchinson of Massachusetts—and, in the case of William Douglass, of the colonies as an entity.

Meanwhile, the air of an American, his manner and interests, made him distinguishable abroad from the Englishman, and his very language, in accent and tone, was becoming distinctive. Thus, as Boswell records, a London shopkeeper recognized an American at once, for, he said: "You speak neither English nor Scotch, but something different from both which I conclude is the language of America." Not only accent and tone were different—new words, borrowed from the Indian and the African, the Dutch and the Swede, the German and the French were pushing their way into everyday American speech.

When, after the Seven Years' War, England turned her efforts towards devising some system of control and exploitation that could be applied at once and uniformly throughout the colonies, she was responding not only to her own needs, but also to the increasing unity in fact of her thirteen colonies. Only this can explain the unity of the resistance to that policy, the immediacy with which a Stamp Act Congress could come into being, and the remark of a Charleston delegate, Christopher Gadsden, to that Congress: "There ought to be no New England men, no New Yorker, etc., known on the continent, but all of us Americans." This puts in conditional terms what Patrick Henry affirmed irrevocably and with some exaggeration in his famous declaration a decade later: "The distinction between Virginians, Pennsylvanians, New Yorkers, and New Englanders, are no more. I am not a Virginian, but an American."

Expressions like these, with the sentiments behind them, and the historically developed reality behind those sentiments, bring us into a new era, that of the American Revolution. On this epoch there is, of course, an enormous literature. But, believing with Mill that, "on all great subjects much remains to be said," perhaps this writer will be forgiven if in a subsequent volume, he adds some pages of his own.

Reference Notes

CHAPTER I

[1] E. P. Cheyney, *European Background of American History: 1300-1600*, author's preface; D. J. Boorstin, *The Americans: The Colonial Experience*, p. 110.

[2] Wesley Frank Craven has aptly written: ". . . even a cursory examination of the records emphasizes the fact that few historians have managed to convey a feeling for the full extent to which the Indian problem absorbed the energies and thought of the colonists"—*The Southern Colonies in the Seventeenth Century*, p. 173n.

CHAPTER II

[1] By the Treaty of Utrecht, ending that war, England obtained Newfoundland, Nova Scotia, and the Hudson's Bay region in present Canada. She also received a monopoly of the slave-carrying trade servicing the Spanish colonies.

CHAPTER III

[1] At this time such English cities as Bristol, Liverpool and Manchester had populations under 30,000.

[2] A law in force from 1664 to 1667, and aimed mostly at Quakers, provided that anyone convicted three times of attending an unlawful religious meeting might be banished to the colonies for a seven-year period; perhaps as many as 100 actually reached the colonies because of this law. Hundreds of Scotch nationalist rebels, however, especially after the uprising of 1679, were sent to the colonies as political criminals. In addition, an act of 1670 provided for the banishment of those who, having knowledge of illegal religious or political activity, refused to turn informers. Some—the number is not known—who resisted self-degradation, were shipped off to the colonies.

[3] Louis B. Wright and Marion Tinling, eds., *The Secret Diary of William Byrd*.

[4] It is to be observed that the exceptional instance of slaves actually freeing themselves by revolt—in Haiti—occurred in a land where they numbered 90% of the total population (with many of the free population being themselves not white) and succeeded while the metropolitan power was itself in revolution.

[5] Several colonies also forbade marriage between free Negro and white—typical was the Maryland law of 1692 providing that a white woman

143

marrying a Negro was to become a servant for seven years; the Negro for life.

⁶ The next century marks the dominance of chattel slavery over indentured servitude in the plantation economy. However, occasional uprisings, occur in the 18th century, as, for example in 1729 in Virginia, when the entire estate of Thomas Lee, the colony's acting governor, was put to the torch by servants.

CHAPTER IV

¹ By 1662, impoverishment was such a problem in Boston that the city built an almshouse. By the 18th century all colonial cities of any size had one or more such "poorhouses."

² An earlier impressment of four New York fishermen into the Royal Navy in 1714, resulted in a popular outbreak and the destruction of a small naval vessel. On the whole subject of impressment as an American colonial grievance, see: Dora Mae Clark, "The impressment of Seamen in the American Colonies," in *Essays in Colonial History Presented to Charles M. Andrews,* pp. 198-244.

³ Tryon's son-in-law, a tax-collector, had been convicted of extortion, but was allowed to go free. This, typifying the rulers' corruption, sparked a Regulator outbreak at Hillsborough, so Tryon had strong personal motivations in leading the suppression. This son-in-law, Edmund Fanning, led a Tory regiment in New York during the Revolution that was notorious for its cruelty.

CHAPTER V

¹ Wrote William Byrd I of Virginia soon after the Revolution of 1689: "When the body is disturbed the members needs be affected; therefore we here can expect no settled times, till England is in peace."

² It is worth noting that Virginia, from 1652 to 1660, was also virtually a self-governing entity, insisting upon the supreme authority of her local organs of rule.

³ The above description of Bacon's Uprising was written before the appearance of Wilcomb E. Washburn's *The Governor and the Rebel: A History of Bacon's Rebellion in Virginia* (published for the Institute of Early American History and Culture at Williamsburg, by the Univ. of North Carolina Press, Chapel Hill 1958). Dr. Washburn's book is another manifestation of the neo-conservatism that has been so marked a feature of American historiography (and ideology, in general) since World War II. Its viewpoint is intensely sympathetic to Governor Berkeley, who is pictured as a man of honor and integrity sincerely concerned with developing legal and moderate reforms; it is altogether hostile to Bacon, who is presented as a demagogic rabble-rouser, obsessed with hatred of Indians and altogether indifferent to proposals for governmental changes. My text has not been altered in any way, upon having read Dr. Washburn's work since I found it singularly unconvincing with its thesis flowing from the *a priori* conceptions of the author and with the evidence, including much of that which

he himself presents, refuting that thesis. Indeed, a new element in Washburn's book is the additional evidence it offers showing that the Bacon movement sprang from very deep and widespread popular discontent, and that this discontent was frequently ahead of Bacon's leadership. Berkeley himself explained the success of the rebels by telling the Royal Commission of Inquiry that of about 15,000 adults in the colony, not 500 were untainted by treason.

CHAPTER VI

[1] British efforts to control the molasses trade (as the Molasses Act of 1733) aroused tremendous colonial opposition, exactly because it was of such transcendant economic significance. This is what John Adams had in mind when he said molasses had been an important ingredient of independence.

CHAPTER VII

[1] It must be added, however, that a class orientation was assumed in most of the writing of the Enlightenment. That is, the submissiveness of the poor to the rich was held to be necessary, else chaos would appear; again, while disbelief in the supernatural was all right for the rich, as Voltaire insisted, he was careful to add that it was dangerous for the poor who, without their fear of and faith in a deity might despair of bearing their burdens and might threaten "civilization." Franklin's view was similar.

[2] Thus, John Knox, founder of Scottish Presbyterianism, who died in 1572, said: "The common song is that we must obey our kings, be they good or bad, for God hath so commanded . . . but it is not less than blasphemy to say God commanded kings to be obeyed when they commanded impiety." On the basis of the same reasoning, the propriety of woman's complete subjection to men was questioned in the writings of Mary Astell, Daniel Defoe and Benjamin Franklin, in the late 17th and early 18th centuries. Franklin also, in his *Reflections on Courtship and Marriage* (1743), questioned the parents' right to force marriage upon youngsters, for authority had to be based upon sound reasoning and moral righteousness in all cases and not simply on power.

CHAPTER VIII

[1] Professor Alan Simpson argues in favor of the Miller view in the *William and Mary Quarterly* (January, 1956), but his presentation is, to me, not persuasive.

[2] This Williams did with greatest clarity in his justly famous work, *The Bloudy Tenent* . . . published in 1644. It was addressed to the English Parliament, which repaid the compliment by ordering the common hangman to burn the book.

[3] Roger Williams, himself, lived long enough to observe this trend and to be troubled by it. In 1664, he wrote to Winthrop's son: ". . . I fear that the common trinity of the world (Profit, Preferment, Pleasure) will here be the *Tria omnia*, as in all the world beside: that Prelacy and Papacy

too will in this wilderness predominate [and] that God Land will be (as now it is) as great a God with us English as God Gold was with the Spanish."

⁴ Another "anarchic" tendency of the time was the appearance of doubts concerning man's innate depravity. Henry Burt, for instance, was prosecuted in the 1640's in Massachusetts for insisting that he was free of sin and that true Christians could live without being sinful.

⁵ That is, *The Great Achievements of Christ in America,* first published in London in 1702.

CHAPTER IX

¹ Perry Miller, in *The American Puritans: Their Prose and Poetry,* p. 122, states that "the revolution Wise proposed in New England thinking had little effect on his contemporaries"; but the impact of his ideas was very great, and his popularity was tremendous. Miller also declares that "Wise was curiously not invoked in the Revolutionary discussion"; but this is plain error, for his work was reproduced just before the Revolution and was well-known to its leaders.

² This was true even of so extreme a sect as the 17th century Quakers, who did win many converts. It is significant, too, that it was popular disgust with and opposition to the Puritan oligarchy's policy of torture and execution of Quakers that helped force its abandonment.

CHAPTER X

¹ Edward Wells, *A Treatise of Ancient and Present Geography* (1701). Half a century later, James Otis bitterly complained that in England, "we are little more known than the savages of California." Professor Thomas A. Bailey has noted: "For a decade the Duke of Newcastle discussed Cape Breton without knowing that it was an island. George III was probably not the only Briton to confuse the Mississippi River with the Ganges in India"—*A Diplomatic History of the American People,* p. 2n.

² R. Hofstadter & W. P. Metzger, *The Development of Academic Freedom in the U.S.,* p. 114.

³ Opening the section, "Along the Road to Revolution," in his *The Pursuit of Science in Revolutionary America* Brooke Hindle wrote (p. 105): "An American sense of destiny—even an American nationalism—had long been developing." Chapter six of the volume is devoted to substantiating this remark, in terms of colonial scientific and cultural life.

⁴ William S. Sachs, "Interurban Correspondents and the Development of a National Economy before the Revolution: New York as a Case Study," in *New York History,* July, 1955.

Bibliography

The historical literature on the colonial period is enormous. What follows is a highly selective listing from that body of work, with emphasis upon those writings which the present author found most suggestive, informative or important.

Contemporaneous materials—so-called "primary" sources—are abundant, including much that is readily accessible in any good-sized public library; among such works are the collected writings of John Adams, Benjamin Franklin, Thomas Jefferson, and George Washington whose early years were spent, of course, as colonials. In addition, again concentrating on works readily available, we would mention:

ANDREWS, CHARLES M., ed., *Narratives of the Insurrections, 1675-1690* (N.Y., 1951, Scribners)

APTHEKER, HERBERT, ed. *A Documentary History of the Negro People in the U.S.* (N.Y., 1951, Citadel)

BOSWELL, JAMES, *Life of Samuel Johnson,* edited by G. B. Hill (London 1934, 6 vols., Oxford Univ.)

COMMAGER, HENRY S., ed., *Documents of American History* (N.Y., 1948, 4th edit., 2 vols. in 1, Appleton-Century-Crofts)

CREVECOEUR, HECTOR, ST. JOHN, *Letters from an American Farmer* (Everyman's Library, 1945)

DONNAN, ELIZABETH, ed., *Documents Illustrative of the History of the Slave Trade to America* (Washington, 1930-35, 4 vols., Carnegie Inst.)

HART, ALBERT B., ed., *American History Told by Contemporaries,* vols. I and II from 1492-1783 (N.Y., 1898, Macmillan)

JENSEN, MERRILL, ed., *American Colonial Documents to 1776,* being vol. IX of *English Historical Documents,* edited by D. C. Douglas (N.Y., 1955 Oxford Univ.)

MILLER, PERRY, ed., *American Puritans: Their Prose and Poetry* (N.Y., 1955, Doubleday)

RUTHERFORD, LIVINGSTON, *John Peter Zenger, His Press, His Trial* (N.Y., 1904). This volume contains verbatim reports of the court proceedings.

THORP, WILLARD, CURTI, MERLE, and BAKER, CARLOS, eds., *American Issues*: Vol. I: *The Social Record* (Phila., 1955, Lippincott, revised and enlarged edit.) This volume contains generous extracts from the writings of Increase Mather, Cotton Mather, Jonathan Edwards, William Penn, John Winthrop, Roger Williams, John Wise, and other outstanding colonial personalities.

WRIGHT, LOUIS B., and TINLING, M., eds. *The Secret Diary of William Byrd . . . 1709-1712* (Richmond, 1941, Dietz)

WRIGHT, LOUIS B., ed., *The Letters of Robert Carter, 1720-1727* (Huntington Library, San Marino, Cal., 1956)

147

During my university days, a most revered teacher was the late Professor Evarts Boutell Greene; it seemed to me then that his learning and the keenness of his judgments were extraordinary. The ensuing years have produced confirmation that my youthful opinion, in this regard, was not in error. And re-examining the literature on the colonial period, in connection with this work, leads me to remark that there is no better guide through many of the areas of that period than the works of Professor Greene, several of which are listed below. In addition, the pages that follow offer a listing of what are believed to be the most significant secondary writings of this era. I have starred those works which, to me, were outstanding in stimulation or information.

ADAMS, JAMES TRUSLOW, *The Founding of New England* (Boston, 1921, Little, Brown)

ADAMS, J. T., *Provincial Society, 1690-1763* (being vol. III of *A History of American Life,* edited by A. Cole, A. Schlesinger and D. Fox, Macmillan, 1927)

ALBION, ROBERT G., *Forests and Sea Power* (Cambridge, 1926, Harvard Univ.)

ALVORD, CLARENCE W., *The Mississippi Valley in British Politics* (2 vols., Cleveland, 1917, A. H. Clark)

*ANDREWS, CHARLES M., *The Colonial Period of American History* (4 vols., New Haven, 1934-38, Yale Univ.)

BALDWIN, ALICE M., *The New England Clergy and the American Revolution* (Durham, 1928, Duke Univ.)

BANCROFT, GEORGE, *History of the United States from the Discovery to the Adoption of the Constitution* (6 vols., N.Y., 1883-85, Appleton), Vols., I, II, III

BEER, GEORGE L., *British Colonial Policy, 1754-1765* (N.Y., 1907, Macmillan)

*BEER, GEORGE L., *The Origins of the British Colonial System, 1578-1660* N.Y., 1909, Macmillan)

BEARD, CHARLES A. and MARY R., *The Rise of American Civilization* (2 vols., in 1, N.Y., 1936, Macmillan)

BENSON, MARY S., *Women in Eighteenth Century America* (N.Y., 1935, Columbia Univ.)

BOND, BEVERLY W., *The Quit-Rent System in the American Colonies* (New Haven, 1919, Yale Univ.)

BOORSTIN, DANIEL J., *The Americans: The Colonial Experience* (N.Y., 1958 Random House)

*BRIDENBAUGH, CARL, *Cities in the Wilderness . . . 1625-1742* (N.Y., 1955, Knopf)

*BRIDENBAUGH, C., *Cities in Revolt . . . 1743-1776* (N.Y., 1955, Knopf)

BRIDENBAUGH, C., *The Colonial Craftsman* (N.Y., 1950, New York Univ.)

BRIDENBAUGH, C., "The Virginians," reprinted in E. SAVETH, ed., *Understanding the American Past* (Boston, 1954, Little, Brown)

BROCKUNIER, SAMUEL, *Irrepressible Democrat: Roger Williams* (N.Y., 1940, Ronald Press)

BROOKES, GEORGE S., *Friend Anthony Benezet* (Phil., 1937, Univ. of Pa.)

BROWN, ROBERT E., *Middle-Class Democracy and the Revolution in Massachusetts, 1691-1780*, (Ithaca, 1955, Cornell Univ.)

BRUCE, KATHLEEN, *Virginia Iron Manufacture in the Slave Era* (N.Y., 1930, Century)

BRUCE, PHILIP A., *Economic History of Virginia in the Seventeenth Century* (2 vols., N. Y., 1896, Macmillan)

BURANELLI, VINCENT, ed., *The Trial of Peter Zenger* (N.Y., 1957, New York Univ.)

CALHOUN, ARTHUR W., *A Social History of the American Family* (3 vols. in 1, N.Y., 1945, Barnes & Noble)

*CHANNING, EDWARD, *A History of the United States* (6 vols., N.Y., 1905-25, Macmillan), vols. I and II

CHEYNEY, EDWARD P., *European Background of American History*, being vol. 1 of *The American Nation: A History*, edited by A. B. Hart (N.Y., 1904, Harper)

CLARK, DORA M., *"The Impressment of Seamen in the American Colonies,"* in *Essays In Colonial History Presented to Charles M. Andrews* (New Haven, 1931, Yale Univ.)

CLOUGH, WILSON O., ed., *Our Long Heritage: Pages from the Books Our Founding Fathers Read* (Minneapolis, 1955, Univ. of Minn.)

COLLIER, JOHN, *Indians of the Americas: The Long Hope* (N.Y., 1948, Mentor)

*COOK, GEORGE A., *John Wise: Early American Democrat* (N.Y., 1952, King's Crown Press)

CRANE, VERNER W., *The Southern Frontier, 1670-1732* (Durham, 1928, Duke Univ.)

CRAVEN, AVERY O., *Soil Exhaustion as a Factor in the Agricultural History of Virginia 1606-1860* (Urbana, 1925, Univ. of Illinois)

CRAVEN, WESLEY F., *The Southern Colonies in the Seventeenth Century*, being vol. I of *A History of the South*, edited by W. H. Stephenson and E. M. Coulter (Baton Rouge, 1949, Louisiana State Univ.)

CROSS, ARTHUR L., *The Anglican Episcopate in the American Colonies* (Cambridge, 1902, Harvard Univ.)

*DOBB, MAURICE, *Studies in the Development of Capitalism* (N.Y., 1947, International)

DORFMAN, JOSEPH, *The Economic Mind in American Civilization* (2 vols., N.Y., 1946, Viking), vol I.

*DuBOIS, W. E. B., *The Suppression of the African Slave Trade to the United States* (originally published by Harvard Univ. Press, 1896, reprinted Social Science Press, N.Y., 1954)

DUNIWAY, CLYDE A., *The Development of Freedom of the Press in Massachusetts* (N.Y., 1906, Longmans Green)

EDWARDS, EVERETT E., *"American Indian Contributions to Civilization,"* in *Minnesota History* (1934, vol. V)

FONER, PHILIP S., *History of the Labor Movement in the United States* (N.Y., 1947, International, vol. I)

*FOSTER, WILLIAM Z., *Outline Political History of the Americas* (N.Y., 1951, International)

FRANK, JOSEPH, *The Levellers* (Cambridge, 1955, Harvard Univ.)

GEWEHR, WESLEY M., *The Great Awakening in Virginia* (Durham, 1930, Duke Univ.)

GOEBEL, JULIUS and NAUGHTON, T. R., *Law Enforcement in Colonial New York* (N.Y., 1944, Columbia Univ.)

GOULD, CLARENCE P., *The Land System in Maryland* (Baltimore, 1913, Johns Hopkins Univ.)

*GRAY, LEWIS H., *History of Agriculture in the Southern United States to 1860* (2 vols., Washington, 1933, Carnegie Inst.)

GREENE, EVARTS B., *Provincial America, 1690-1740* (being vol. 6 of *The American Nation: A History*, edited by A. B. HART, N.Y., 1905, Harper)

*GREENE, E. B., *The Foundation of American Nationality* (N.Y., 1935, rev. edit., American Book)

GREENE, E. B., *Religion and the State: The Making and Testing of an American Tradition* (N.Y., 1941, New York Univ.)

GREENE, E. B., and V. D. HARRINGTON, *American Population Before the Federal Census of 1790* (N.Y., 1932, Columbia Univ.)

GREENE, LORENZO J., *The Negro in Colonial New England* (N.Y., 1942, Columbia Univ.)

HALL, W. L., ed., *The Vestry Book of the Upper Parish, Nansemond County, Virginia, 1743-1793* (Richmond, 1949, Dietz)

HARPER, LAWRENCE A., *The English Navigation Laws: A Seventeenth Century Experiment in Social Engineering* (N.Y., 1939, Columbia Univ.)

HARRISON, F., *Virginia Land Grants* (Richmond, 1925, privately printed)

HECKSCHER, E. F., *Mercantilism* (2 vols., London, 1935, G. Allen)

HEDGES, JAMES B., *The Browns of Providence Plantations: Colonial Years* (Cambridge, 1952, Harvard Univ.)

HILDRETH, RICHARD, *The History of the United States of America* (6 vols. rev. edit., vol. I and II)

HILL, CHRISTOPHER, ed., *The English Revolution* (London, 1941, Lawrence & Wishart)

*HILL, C., *Economic Problems of the Church: From Archbishop Whitgift to the Long Parliament* (London, 1955, Oxford Univ.)

HILL, C., "Hobbes and English Political Thought," in R. SELLARS, V. McGILL, M. FARBER, eds., *Philosophy for the Future*, pp. 13-22 (N.Y., 1949, Macmillan)

HINDLE, BROOKE, *The Pursuit of Science in Revolutionary America, 1735-1789* (Chapel Hill, 1956, Univ. of N.C.)

HOFSTADTER, RICHARD and METZGER, W. P., *The Development of Academic Freedom in the United States* (N.Y., 1955, Columbia Univ.)

INNIS, HAROLD, *The Cod Fisheries* (New Haven, 1940, Yale Univ.)

*JERNEGAN, MARCUS L., *Laboring and Dependent Classes in Colonial America* (Chicago, 1931, Univ. of Chicago)

JOHNSON, EMORY R., et al., *History of Domestic and Foreign Commerce of the United States* (2 vols., Washington, 1915, Carnegie Inst.)

JONES, HOWARD M., *The Pursuit of Happiness* (Cambridge, 1953, Harvard Univ.)

KARRAKER, CYRUS H., *Piracy Was a Business* (N.Y., 1953, R. R. Smith)

KEMMERER, D. L., *Path to Freedom: The Struggle for Self-Government in Colonial New Jersey, 1703-1776* (Princeton, 1940, Princeton Univ.)

KITTREDGE, GEORGE L., *Witchcraft in Old and New England* (Cambridge, 1929, Harvard Univ.)

KLINGBERG, FRANK J., *The Morning of America* (N.Y., 1941, Appleton-Century)

LABAREE, LEONARD W., *Conservatism in Early American History* (N.Y., 1948, New York Univ.)

*MARK, IRVING, *Agrarian Conflicts in Colonial New York, 1711-1775* (N.Y., 1940, Columbia Univ.)

McCORMAC, EUGENE I., *Colonial Opposition to Imperial Authority During the French and Indian War* (Berkeley, 1911, Univ. of California.)

McKINLEY, ALBERT E., *The Suffrage Franchise in the Thirteen English Colonies in America* (Phila., 1905, Univ. of Pa.)

MILLER, PERRY, *The New England Mind: The Seventeenth Century* (Cambridge, 1954, Harvard Univ.)

MILLER, P., *Roger Williams* (Indianapolis, 1953, Bobbs-Merrill)

MORAIS, HERBERT M., *Deism in Eighteenth Century America* (N.Y., 1934, Columbia Univ.)

*MORAIS, H. M., *The Struggle for American Freedom: The First Two Hundred Years* (N.Y., 1944, International)

MORISON, SAMUEL E., "The Puritan Tradition," in E. SAVETH, ed., *Understanding the American Past* (Boston, 1954, Little, Brown)

MORRIS, RICHARD B., ed., *The Era of the American Revolution* (N.Y., 1939, Columbia Univ.)

*MORRIS, R. B., *Government and Labor in Early America* (N.Y., 1946, Columbia Univ.)

MORSE, JARVIS M., *American Beginnings* (Washington, 1952, Public Affairs Press)

McKEE, S., *Labor in Colonial New York, 1664-1776* (N.Y., 1935, Columbia)

NETTELS, CURTIS P., "The Menace of Colonial Manufacturing, 1690-1720," in *New England Quarterly* (April, 1931), IV, pp. 230-69

*NETTELS, C. P., *The Money Supply of the American Colonies Before 1720* (Madison, 1934, Univ. of Wisc.)

*NETTELS, C. P., *The Roots of American Civilization* (N.Y., 1938, Crofts)

NOTESTEIN, WALLACE, *The English People on the Eve of Colonization: 1606-1630*, being a volume in *The New American Nation Series*, edited by H. S. COMMAGER and R. B. MORRIS (N.Y., 1954, Harper)

*OSGOOD, HERBERT L., *The American Colonies in the Seventeenth Century* (2 vols., N.Y., 1904, Columbia Univ.)

*OSGOOD, H. L., *The American Colonies in the Eighteenth Century* (N.Y., 1924, Columbia Univ.)

*PARRINGTON, VERNON L., *Main Currents in American Thought;* Vol. I: *The Colonial Mind* (3 vols., in 1, N.Y., c. 1930, Harcourt, Brace)

PECKHAM, H. H., *Pontiac and the Indian Uprising* (Princeton, 1947, Princeton Univ.)

PERRY, RALPH B., *Puritanism and Democracy* (N.Y., 1944, Vanguard)

REICH, JEROME R., *Leisler's Rebellion* (Chicago, 1953, Univ. of Chicago)

Root, W. T., *The Relations of Pennsylvania with the British Government* (Philadelphia, 1912, Univ. of Pa.)

*Rossiter, Clinton, *Seedtime of the Republic: The Origin of the American Tradition of Political Liberty* (N.Y., 1953, Harcourt, Brace)

Rourke, Constance, *The Roots of American Culture, and Other Essays,* ed., by Van Wyck Brooks (N.Y., 1942, Harcourt)

Sachs, William S., "Interurban Correspondence and the Development of a National Economy before the Revolution: New York as a Case Study," in *New York History* (July, 1955), XXXVI, pp. 320-35

*Savelle, Max, *Seeds of Liberty: The Genesis of the American Mind* (N.Y., 1948, Knopf)

Scott, W. R., *The Constitution and Finance of English, Scottish, and Irish Joint Stock Companies* (3 vols., Cambridge, 1910-12, Cambridge Univ.)

Seidman, A. B., "Church and State in the Early Years of the Massachusetts Bay Colony," in *The New England Quarterly* (June, 1945), XVIII, pp. 211-33

Simpson, Alan, "How Democratic Was Roger Williams?" in *William & Mary Quarterly* (Jan. 1956), 3rd ser., XIII, pp. 53-67

Sly, John F., *Town Government in Massachusetts* (Cambridge, 1930, Harvard Univ.)

*Smith, Abbot E., *Colonists in Bondage: White Servitude and Convict Labor in America, 1607-1776* (Chapel Hill, 1947, Univ. of N.C.)

Spruill, Julia C., *Women's Life and Work in the Southern Colonies* (Chapel Hill, 1936, Univ. of N.C.)

Starkey, Marion L., *The Devil in Massachusetts,* (N.Y., 1949, Knopf)

Struik, Dirk L., *Yankee Science in the Making* (Boston, 1948, Little, Brown)

Sweet, William W., *The Story of Religion in America* (N.Y., 1950, 2nd rev. edit., Harper)

Sweet, W. W., *Religion in Colonial America* (N.Y., 1953, Scribner's)

Tolles, Frederick B., *Meeting House and Counting House: The Quaker Merchants of Colonial Philadelphia, 1682-1763* (Chapel Hill, 1948, Univ. of N.C.)

*Tyler, Moses C., *A History of American Literature, 1607-1765,* (c. 1878, reissued, Ithaca, 1949, Cornell Univ.)

Van Doren, Carl, *Benjamin Franklin* (N.Y., 1938, Viking)

Washburn, Wilcomb E., *The Governor and the Rebel: A History of Bacon's Rebellion in Virginia* (Chapel Hill, 1958, Univ. of N.C.)

Wertenbaker, Thomas J., *Torchbearer of the Revolution* (Princeton, 1940, Princeton Univ.)

Wertenbaker, T. J., *The Founding of American Civilization: The Middle Colonies* (N.Y., 1940, Scribners)

Wertenbaker, T. J., *The Old South: The Founding of American Civilization* (N.Y., 1942, Scribners)

Winslow, Ola E., *Jonathan Edwards, 1703-1758* (N. Y., 1940, Macmillan)

Winslow, O. E., *Meetinghouse Hill: 1630-1783* (N.Y., 1952, Macmillan)

Bibliography   153

*WINSLOW, O.E., *Master Roger Williams* (N.Y., 1957, Macmillan)
*WISH, HARVEY, *Society and Thought in Early America* (N.Y., 1950, Longmans Green)
WILLIAMSON, A. S., *Credit Relations between Colonial and English Merchants in the 18th Century* (Iowa City, 1932, Univ. of Iowa)
WRIGHT, LOUIS B., *The Atlantic Frontier: Colonial American Civilization* (N.Y., 1947, Knopf)
ZEICHNER, OSCAR, *Connecticut's Years of Controversy* (Chapel Hill, 1949, Univ. of N.C.)

In addition, certain local histories offer important information not always available elsewhere. Among the many examples, may be mentioned:

LEE, FRANCIS B., *New Jersey as a Colony and as a State* (4 vols., N.Y. 1902, Pub. Soc. of N.J.)
LINCOLN, WILLIAM, *History of Worcester, Mass.* (Worcester, 1862, Hersey)
MORGAN, FORREST, *Connecticut as a Colony and as a State* (3 vols., Hartford, 1904, Pub. Soc. of Conn.)

I have drawn on certain of my earlier writings for some of the material in this volume. These include:
American Negro Slave Revolts (N.Y., 1943, Columbia Univ.)
To Be Free: Studies in American Negro History (N.Y., 1948, International)
Toward Negro Freedom (N.Y., 1956, New Century)

ADDITIONAL BIBLIOGRAPHY

BARROW, THOMAS C., "Background to the Grenville Program, 1757-1763," *William and Mary Quarterly* (January, 1965), XXII, 93-104
BILLIAS, GEORGE A., ed., *Law and Authority in Colonial America: Selected Essays* (Barre, Mass., 1965, Barre Publishers)
ELLIS, JOHN T., *Catholics in Colonial America* (Baltimore, 1965, Helicon)
GREENE, JACK P., *The Quest for Power: The Lower Houses of Assembly in the Southern Royal Colonies, 1689-1776* (Chapel Hill, 1963, Univ. of N.C.)
HENRETTA, JAMES A., "Economic Development and Social Structure in Colonial Boston," *William and Mary Quarterly* (January, 1965) XXII, 75-92
LEDER, LAWRENCE H., *Robert Livingston, 1654-1728, and the Politics of Colonial New York* (Chapel Hill, 1961, Univ. of N.C.)
LEE, LAWRENCE, *The Lower Cape Fear* [N.C.] *in Colonial Days* (Chapel Hill, 1965, Univ. of N.C.)
MIDDLEKAUF, ROBERT, *Ancients and Axioms: Secondary Education in Eighteenth-Century New England* (New Haven, 1963, Yale Univ.)
MORGAN, EDMUND S., *The Gentle Puritan: A Life of Ezra Stiles, 1727-1795* (New Haven, 1962, Yale Univ.)
MORGAN, EDMUND S., *Visible Saints: The History of a Puritan Idea* (N.Y., 1963, N.Y. Univ.)

Nash, Gary B., "The Framing of Government in Pennsylvania: Idea in Contact with Reality," *William and Mary Quarterly* (April, 1966), XXIII, 183-209

Peckham, Howard H., *The Colonial Wars, 1689-1762* (Chicago, 1964, Univ. of Chicago)

Powell, Sumner C., *Puritan Village: The Formation of a New England Town* [Sudbury, Mass.] (Middletown, Conn., 1963, Wesleyan Univ.)

Rutnam, D. B., *Winthrop's Boston: Portrait of a Puritan Town* (Chapel Hill, 1965, Univ. of N.C.)

Towner, L. W., "The Sewall-Saffin Dialogue on Slavery [1700-1701]" *William and Mary Quarterly* (January, 1964), XXI, 40-52

Ver Steeg, Clarence L., *The Formative Years, 1607-1763* (N.Y., 1964, Hill & Wang)

Index